NON-FICTION 372.41 LEONHARD
Leonhardt, Mary.
Parents who love reading,
kids who don't : how it
happens and what you can do
about it / Mary Leonhardt.
1st ed.

NO 19'93	DATE DUE		
NO 27'93			
DE 7'93			
JA 02'94			
FE 10'94			
AP 9'94			
AP 24'94			
JE 20'94			

Parents

who love reading,

Kids who don't

PARENTS

WHO LOVE READING,

KIDS

WHO DON'T

---

*How It Happens
and What You
Can Do About It*

MARY LEONHARDT

Crown Publishers, Inc.

New York

Published by Crown Publishers, Inc.
201 East 50th Street, New York, New York 10022
Member of the Crown Publishing Group.

Random House, Inc. New York, Toronto, London, Sydney, Auckland

CROWN is a trademark of Crown Publishers, Inc.

Manufactured in the United States of America

Library of Congress Cataloging-in-Publication Data

Leonhardt, Mary.
    Parents who love reading, kids who don't : how it happens and what you can do about it / Mary Leonhardt. — 1st ed.
        p.   cm.
    Includes index.
    1. Reading—United States—Parent participation.   2. Children—United States—Books and reading.   3. Education—United States—Parent participation.   I. Title.
    LB1050.L456   1993
    372.41—dc20   93-16655
                                                            CIP

ISBN 0-517-59164-2

10 9 8 7 6 5 4 3 2 1

First edition

This book is dedicated to the thousands of kids who hate reading:

"When I was in elementary school I hated to read. The other kids just always seemed more advanced than me. Teachers often criticized my reading and made me feel like I was stupid. I was never reading enough for them, or maybe I was reading too slow. They also wanted me to read what they thought I should be reading, they didn't care about what I had to say or what my interests were. They sometimes would call my parents and tell them that I had a reading problem. Before I knew it, it seemed as though I was being forced to read. Reading soon became a punishment rather than a pleasure. I hated reading!"

A boy in my sophomore class

CONTENTS

ACKNOWLEDGMENTS

Thanks to Everyone Who Helped Me:

My mother—for giving me her love of reading
My father—for showing me what an avid reader could accomplish
My husband—for believing in me and supporting me
My children—for teaching me everything important I know about life
My students—for teaching me everything important I know about education

Especially those who helped with this book:
All of my students, over the years, for their book evaluations, but especially: Susan Passus for her help with Danielle Steel; Frank Kreiger, Don Brown, Greg Doran, and Ed Schriener for their help with the sports books; Steve Furneaux, Ben Garwood, Mark Anderson, Chris Harkins, Pete Henry, Chris Hazelton, and James Dolberg for their help with the science fiction/fantasy section; Kristin and Carrie Finno, Laura and Sarah Hearn, Molly Leonhardt, Ben Kissinger, and Mary Alice Barron, who helped with the juvenile sections, and Josh Henry, who helped with the comic section. A special thank you to Patrick Twoomy for the most entertaining comments (see evaluations of Vonnegut, LeCarré, and Waugh). A special thanks to *all* my students of the 1991–92 and 1992–93 school years.

Thanks to Lenore Henry and Nancy Finno, my honest first readers of this manuscript.

Thanks to Jim Fitzgerald, who gave me the courage to write this book.

PARENTS

WHO LOVE READING,

KIDS WHO DON'T

————————————

TWENTY YEARS AGO, WHEN I RECEIVED MY MA IN ENG-lish from Brown University, I was sure I knew why some teenagers read so much better than others. They came from good families. Their parents had read to them as children. They grew up surrounded by books. Of course they loved reading and were good readers.

Then I started teaching, and things no longer looked so simple.

I was teaching in a private Dominican boarding school in California. The girls came from wonderful homes, but a dis-turbing number weren't avid readers; some didn't like to read at all. I was at a complete loss. I knew how to run a Chaucer seminar . . . but teach reading? I thought there was some specialized knowledge that I didn't have.

Following my navy husband, I moved on to Virginia. He went to sea, and I taught in a couple of different high schools while beginning a graduate program in learning dis-abilities at Old Dominion University. I was lucky at Old Dominion, having a visiting professor from the University of Chicago, Ken James, who had trained under Doris John-son, one of the people who helped define the field. His axiom: a diagnosis of learning disabilities is a diagnosis of last resort. Consider it only when there is no other possible reason for the reading failure.

After twenty years of teaching English and really paying attention to my poor readers, I concur with him. I have, at the most, a handful of kids every year who I think are truly learning disabled . . . and by high school age most of them have learned to compensate.

So what is causing the massive dislike and avoidance of reading that I see in the majority of my high school students? Except for a handful of cases, I'm sure it's not learning disabilities. What are the reading specialists saying?

I see reading specialists either looking for very esoteric, complicated reasons ("He has trouble with the sequencing of ideas") or blaming the environment of the student. If older children, or teenagers, don't like to read, it must be because their parents don't like to read, or their parents didn't read to them when they were little, or there weren't any books in their home.

And yet, after twenty years of teaching, I can't count the number of parents who say wistfully to me, "I can't understand why he won't read. Everyone else in the family loves to read. We've read to him since he was a baby." A very good friend of mine sadly explained to me why she thought one of her three sons didn't like to read. "He was the middle one," she told me. "I guess I just didn't have as much time to sit down and read to him. His brothers love to read, but I guess I shortchanged him somehow."

I understand her feeling because, when my second child, Tim, was also very slow to catch on to reading, I wondered for years what I had done wrong. Heaven knows I had loved him and read to him. The bookcase in his room was overflowing with all the Richard Scarry books, the Curious George books, and countless others. And he *did* love books when he started school. But he went through elementary school and junior high in the lowest reading groups. He received special education services until he was in ninth grade. Needless to say, by that time he had come to see reading as drudgery.

But I'm through feeling guilty. Now I'm angry. After paying attention to my students, and my own children, for the last twenty years, I'm convinced that the education establishment is primarily responsible for the endemic dislike of reading among kids.

I discovered something else over these years, though. I discovered many ways to turn around a dislike for reading. I became the reading fanatic in any school in which I taught. My classrooms have always been full of books. Currently, in my classroom in Concord, Massachusetts, I have hundreds of paperbacks on my shelves, and hundreds more stored in cupboards underneath. I'll do almost anything to get students reading.

That's what this book is primarily about. It will tell you how to rekindle in your son or daughter a love of reading. You read to them when they were small. You sent them off to school with fond memories of *The Cat in the Hat* and *The Lorax*. (Invariably, when I ask my students who are poor readers for the title of a book they have liked, some will give me a children's title, like *Green Eggs and Ham*. I guess it was the last book they can remember enjoying.) And then you watched as their love of reading dwindled away, and reading became a disagreeable chore.

It's never too late to help your son or daughter regain a love of reading. I will explain in this book what kind of attitude works best with reluctant readers, what kinds of books and magazines will help them get started again, how you can help navigate their school career to prevent further damage. Over the years, I've watched hundreds of my students fall in love with reading again.

I've also been, incredibly, lucky enough to watch my own son regain a love of reading. Tim was a child who entered third grade not reading at all. Now he's a college student. I had to take him up to the University of Maine a day early this fall because he was invited to join the humanities honors program. I think it was all the reading he did in high school that finally made this possible. For the last three or four years he's always had some book going. When we moved, a year ago, he insisted on hand-carrying some of his books; he was afraid the movers might lose them.

Your child, too, can fall in love with reading again. I'll first explain why avid reading is so important, and why so many students are not avid readers. Next I'll coach you on how to develop avid-reading behavior in your child. And finally, I'll give you advice on the kind of school to choose, and the way to deal with common school problems, particularly the problems low-level readers have.

1

How Important Is It That Your Child Be An Avid Reader?

I'M SURE THAT, SINCE YOU LOVE READING YOURSELF, YOU have a strong sense of why reading is so important. It adds depth to our lives. It fills many otherwise lonely or boring hours with excitement and pleasure. It helps us make sense out of our world.

What you may not completely understand is the overwhelming difference between an avid reader and a person who rarely reads for pleasure. Since I'm going to suggest later that you do some things you might not really approve of—such as encourage your child to read fairly junky subliterature—it's important that you understand the crucial importance of avid reading. The following observations are drawn from my twenty years of teaching experience, in public, private, and parochial schools all over the country.

Only Avid Readers Are Excellent Readers

A little quiz: How do children become fast, fluent, sophisticated readers?

A. They do lots of phonics work sheets, read carefully through a basal reading series, and spend much time memorizing vocabulary.
B. They do all their schoolwork and occasionally read a good classic children's book selected by a parent or librarian.
C. Their reading often, or even always, consists of subliterature—like comic books, horror novels, science fiction, or romances. They may or may not do their schoolwork. But they read constantly.

The answer, of course, is C. Good readers *are* good readers only because they read all the time. The fact that much, or even all, of their reading is of rather questionable literary value doesn't seem to matter, at least until they reach high school age. By high school age, if they have been avidly reading since elementary school, they often move on to more complex, satisfying literature—"layered literature," one of my students calls it. But it's the early reading that they've done that allows them to enjoy more difficult books.

The boarding school in California where I first taught was an excellent school, and many of the students went on to very prestigious colleges. One of my students wanted to go to Stanford. Her parents had gone there, she was an excellent, hardworking student—but she wasn't an avid reader. In her junior year she took the college board exam and only scored 500 on the verbal section. That score was probably going to keep her out of Stanford. The principal asked me if I would tutor her.

Well, I did tutor her a little, but then I thought to ask her about reading. What kind of reading did she do as a child? "Not much," she told me. "My mother said Nancy Drew and the other books I liked were trash. She used to read me Henry James." Aha!

Since this was a boarding school, and there was no mother around to criticize, I talked her into trying *The Flame and the Flower* by Kathleen Woodiwiss. Well! My student had had no idea that books could be like this! (I think "bodice ripper" is the technical term for Woodiwiss-style page-turners.) Anyway, my student went on to read her next book, *The Wolf and the Dove*, and from then on was thoroughly hooked. She spent the end of her junior year and much of her senior year walking around with some very engrossing historical romance in her hand. And when she retook the college boards a year later her verbal score had gone up a whole 100 points, and she was accepted at Stanford. "I owe it all to trashy books!" she told me.

Actually, the books don't have to be "trashy"—my student's word for mass market fiction—as long as they are absolutely engrossing. I'm convinced that any kind of reading, as long as students find it enthralling, will quickly and significantly raise reading levels.

Consider what techniques are taught in reading improvement courses. You're taught to look at the whole piece of writing first to get a framework. You're taught to read at different rates of speed, depending on the material. You're taught to read with questions in your mind, so you more adequately process the material. When reading something very engrossing a reader does all this automatically.

Before picking up a book, avid readers usually have a good idea what it's about, since they tend to go on reading binges—they'll read all of one author, maybe countless books in one genre. They have a good sense of typical book structures. They read at different rates of speed, because they've trained themselves to rush through, or skip, parts they think are boring, like description. They'll slow down for the good parts, maybe reading them over and over. And, of course, a book that is engrossing to them is continually raising questions in their mind. Who is the murderer? Will the spacemen make it to Mars?

Poor readers, by contrast, have little sense of book structure. They just haven't read enough to acquire it. They read
the whole book, if they ever read a book, at the same slow,
plodding rate of speed. They have trouble anticipating
events and asking questions; they get confused very easily.

But if they once start reading, it's amazing how soon some
of these skills fall into place. An engrossing page-turner simply pulls these skills out of them. They find themselves
pushing to read faster and faster, to find out what's going to
happen. Suddenly they're skipping the boring parts.
They're more alert to what's going on. Kids tell me in wonder, "I couldn't stop reading!" It's a very new, wonderful
experience for them.

In Norfolk, Virginia, I taught at a diocesan Catholic high
school for four years. It was a wonderful school. The philosophy was that if Christ were alive today he wouldn't just
say, "Feed the hungry." He'd say, "Teach the illiterate."
We took in many inner-city kids with extremely low reading
levels. The incoming ninth-graders who tested below a sev-
enth- or eighth-grade reading level were put into a special
saturation reading program. The idea was to quickly raise
their reading levels to a point where they could reenter regular English classes.

We typically started with two classes of ninth-graders,
with kids whose reading levels averaged about fourth or fifth
grade. By tenth grade we were down to one remedial class,
and we had to combine the eleventh- and twelfth-graders
to get one small class. All of the other students attained
reading levels that allowed them to succeed in regular
classes—without any special ed. help, I might add. These
were the days in Virginia, the midseventies, when the state
was just beginning to attempt to comply with the Federal
Special Education Law (PL 94–142). The private and parochial schools were very far from having anything remotely
resembling special ed. resource rooms.

So how did we achieve this minor miracle?

The principal gave me some money—maybe thirty dollars a month—and I scoured Norfolk for out-of-date magazines and comics and paperbacks. We kept this reading material in a big cupboard in my classroom, and when these saturation reading classes came into my room, the kids would go to the cupboard, choose something to read, and then sit and read for the entire period. Sometimes they did a little writing, also—and if I were still doing the program I would put much more writing into it—but mostly they just read. We tested the students frequently, with an individual reading test (the Peabody Picture Reading Test), and found that we got an average gain of eighteen months in reading skills for every six months we had them in this program.

Maybe this doesn't sound like a lot, but consider: if a student enters ninth grade reading on a fourth-grade, fifth-month level, he's been gaining at only half the rate of the student population in general. All of a sudden, by reading very engrossing reading material of his own choice, for only five forty-five-minute periods a week, he is gaining at *three times* the rate of the average student.

The students who were very poor readers coming in, those at a second-grade level, for instance, gained skills much more slowly. But I can't think of any students, in the four years I taught there, who didn't gain any reading skills at all. The kids who came in on a sixth- or seventh-grade level very quickly shot up to a ninth- or tenth-grade level. When students became able to engross themselves in reading material, their scores generally started to climb pretty rapidly. I find that the ability of a student to engross himself in reading material is the most important skill to look for in poor readers.

The other day, in the public school in Concord, Massachusetts I now teach in, a special ed. teacher explained to me that one of my students had scored very low on a reading comprehension test. This was a minority student from Bos-

ton who attends Concord as part of the METCO program—
a state program to bring African-American and Hispanic
students from the inner city to suburban school districts.
This student was in the tenth grade but had scored a little
under a fourth-grade reading level. The teacher told me
about the reading level but then added in a puzzled voice
that she wasn't sure the test was accurate because he
seemed to rush through it. She finally figured out that he
was in such a hurry because he wanted to go back to reading
the book he was reading for me, *Early Autumn* by Robert
Parker.

I was really tickled. His rush to get back to *Early Autumn*
gave me a lot of hope for this young man. I *knew* he was a
poor reader, but now I could keep feeding him Robert Parker books for the rest of the semester, and we'd raise his
reading level pretty quickly.

Good readers *are* good readers because they love reading.
Poor readers—except for the very few who are truly learning disabled—are poor readers because they dislike reading
and never do it unless forced. And forcing them is rarely
effective.

Only Avid Readers
Are Excellent Writers

Compare these two descriptions of the book *A Separate
Peace* by John Knowles.

> This is a book about two boys growing up in
> private school. It deals with their jealousy about
> each other and how they cope with their problems.

This description was written by a very hardworking, conscientious, fifteen-year-old girl who was not, however, an
avid reader. The following description was also written by
a fifteen-year-old girl, but this student loved reading.

> A *Separate Peace* by John Knowles is about a
> friendship between two schoolboys overshadowed
> by World War II and their private one-sided war
> over mistaken jealousy. It is effective because of
> its quiet seriousness and sustained tension.

The second student is light-years ahead of the first in a
number of areas. Notice sentence structure. The first writer
uses only short, declarative sentences. The second writer
opens with a complex sentence containing a participial
phrase with a compound prepositional phrase. She uses another compound prepositional phrase in her second sentence. Yet in spite of the complexity of her sentence
structure, her writing has an easy, effortless flow to it. Not
so with the first writer. Her second sentence, even though
short, sounds awkward and clumsy, because she has no
sense of parallel construction.

Now notice the content of the paragraphs. In twenty-
seven words the first writer doesn't tell us very much. She
says the book is about two boys "growing up in private
school." It sounds as if the book covers a considerable
amount of time—time for the boys to grow up—but in fact
it only covers one school year. She probably means that the
boys had to grow up very quickly in that one year, but she
isn't clear. When she continues with, "It deals with their
jealousy about each other and how they cope with their
problems," she leaves us wondering about what problems,
other than jealousy, they are coping with.

In just thirty-seven words the second writer gives us not
only a crystal clear sense of the plot but makes an astute
comment on the book's tone and pace. She also hints at the
major theme, that is, the boys' private war is affected very
much by the major war their country is fighting.

What causes one student to be able to write and think so
much more clearly than another? I think most people would
just assume that the second writer was more intelligent than

the first, but I disagree. In many areas of life, the first student showed much more intelligence than the second. The first was a brilliant athlete, very astute about social situations, and altogether very competent about organizing her life. The second student wasn't nearly as smart about social situations, had no talent for athletics, and wasn't even that good in abstract subjects like math. But she loved reading. Regency romances, as I remember, were her favorite books. And I think this avid reading *developed* this wonderful verbal intelligence and insight she had. The last time I saw her, she told me she had just graduated from Yale with an A average in her double major of English and Medieval French Literature.

I've described these two students in some detail, because I think they highlight the yawning gulf in writing ability between students with a passion for books and students who only read what they have to. When I first started teaching, I used to try directly to teach the kind of fluency and style that the second writer had. And, actually, trying to teach this fluency is very much in style now. There are whole books and classes that feature sentence-combining exercises. I just haven't found these exercises to work.

I think this is why. Try an experiment. See if you can find a preschool child, around three or four, and ask him to repeat this sentence: "If I were to go to Boston, I would buy you a new coat."

I can almost guarantee you that the child will say something like: "I'll go to Boston and buy you a new coat." The child changes the sentence because your version contains a conditional phrase, with a verb in the subjunctive mood. Few preschoolers have acquired this construction, and children can't even *repeat* a sentence construction that they haven't yet acquired.

When this was pointed out to me, in a course I took on oral language development, I could hardly believe it. But at the time my oldest daughter, who was five, was in a play at school and I found, when trying to teach her the lines, that there were some lines she simply couldn't learn. She couldn't even *say* them, because they contained sophisticated sentence constructions that she had not yet acquired in her everyday speech.

So then we come to the question, how do children acquire language constructions?

Think of a two-year-old now. When it's time for a two-year-old to go to bed, a parent often hears, "Go bed, no!" Think back to that weary, exhilarating time in your life. Did you say, "Oh, honey, you need to embed your negative. Say, 'I don't want to go to bed'"?

Of course not. You gently picked up the little rebel and said, cheerfully and firmly, "But it's bedtime! Now do you want to sleep with Owl tonight, or Jimmy Raccoon, or . . . "

The point is, we respond to what a child *says*, not how he says it. We continually surround children with oral language. From the day they are born we are talking almost nonstop to them. "And now it's time to get that diaper on! That's right, and here's the powder!" The child is two months old. What does he know about powder? But he's picking up language cadence, and tone, and by a year most children have an extremely large receptive language vocabulary. And they are practicing talking. They lie in their crib and coo, and talk that wonderful baby jargon. By a year of age they've perfectly acquired the *sound* of their language. We're sure, if we could just listen closely enough to the jargon, we could understand what they're saying.

Small children also want to hear language and often require you to talk to them. When my son was two, he used to sit in his car seat as I drove to school, and shout to me all the time, "Mommy, truck! Truck! Look, truck!" He wouldn't stop until I said, "Yes, yes, Tim. I see it. You're right. It's a truck!" He'd sit back, satisfied then, until: "Mommy, a car! Look, a car!" He did this for the whole year. He elicited the correct form from me. I never taught him to say, "It's a truck," but he acquired the construction from continually hearing me say it—from continually *making* me say it!

And I figured out why my three-year-old daughter said "why" all the time. We'd pass a tennis court, and she'd say, "What's that?" "That's a tennis court, Julie." Then inevitably she'd say, "Why?" At first I was frustrated. "I don't know! It's just a tennis court!" But then I realized her "why" was just her unsophisticated way of trying to keep the conversation going. So I'd say, "Well, you play a game on it. You hit this ball back and forth." "Why, Mommy?" "You use tennis rackets, and the ball is small, and . . . " And so on.

I can still remember Professor Ken James, at Old Dominion University, saying in our language development course, "A child will perfectly acquire oral language by the age of three-and-a-half. Everything after that is polish." We are very successful at having children acquire oral language because we saturate them with it from the day they are born.

Most children, unfortunately, are not saturated with reading in school, and so never acquire the sophistication and fluency with written language that they have with oral language. The writing of an avid reader jumps off the page at you. In construction, tone, idea formation, style, it's radically different from the writing of a student who rarely reads. It's almost like comparing a two-year-old's "Go bed, no!" with an eight-year-old who explains in great detail to you that yes, of course he will go to bed shortly, but unfortunately his teacher has required that the whole class watch *Hulk IV* on HBO. I'm sure you get the idea.

I think what's actually happening is that poor readers write oral language rather than written language. Oral language and written language are very different. We use much looser grammatical structures when we talk—more compound sentences, plenty of fragments, few complex sentences. Plus, of course, we don't have to punctuate or spell when we talk. Students whose main language input is oral language will write these same loose, slightly awkward structures. They haven't been exposed to enough written language—saturated with enough written language—to acquire sophisticated written-language structures. And, of course, they don't punctuate or spell very adeptly.

This is a typical bit of writing from a nonenthusiastic reader: "I don't read alot on my own. Only if I'm in the mood or have to go on a long trip." Notice the misspelling, the sentence fragment. She's writing oral language.

I'll close with this piece of writing from an excellent reader. She was only fifteen when she wrote this, but note the easy fluency, the humor, and her control of tone:

> Everyone liked Katie. She was funny and friendly, and she seemed absolutely incapable of being mean to anyone. She had so many friends that I wondered how she even kept track of them all. And that's why I hated her so much.

Avid Readers Concentrate on Outside Information and Ideas More Easily

Visit an English class with me called Contemporary Literature. It's an elective for juniors and seniors and has a very mixed group of students in it. Some are excellent, avid readers; some tell me they rarely, or never, read a book unless forced.

We're reading *One Flew Over the Cuckoo's Nest* by Ken Kesey. It's a book that's fairly complicated, because the narrator, the Chief, is an unreliable narrator. He hallucinates much of the time, and the reader has to figure out what part of the story is the Chief's hallucinations and what part is real.

The hallucinations are very funny, and much of the class, those who are competent readers, really enjoy the book. Students who are mediocre to poor readers have a difficult time with this book, so we spend a lot of class time talking about what happens in it.

Here's the irony. The students who readily understand the book follow the class discussions with great interest. They want to talk about how mental illness is portrayed. They want to talk about shock treatment and depression.

The less competent readers—those who really need the class discussions to understand the book—tune the discussions out. The girls will try to talk quietly until I glare at them. They may even try to bring out fingernail polish and do their nails. The guys squirm around restlessly, looking out the window, maybe scribbling on their notebooks.

The difference in ability to pay attention and follow lectures and discussion is so great between excellent readers and poor readers that I've finally decided the two must be correlated. I've seen it in every school, in every classroom I've ever taught in. Avid readers follow discussions closely, even when they don't choose to jump in. They rarely miss anything that goes on in a classroom. Poor readers miss almost everything. It's much harder to hold their attention. Unless the discussion specifically relates to issues they personally find very interesting, we lose them.

My guess is that avid reading *develops* the student's ability to concentrate on verbal information.

Our only heavy input of pure verbal information, outside of classrooms or lectures, is found in books. All other learning experiences—sports, social situations, movies, television, jobs—involve other senses, most notably the visual. To follow a purely oral argument is hard for students who haven't done much reading.

I'm not sure how this ties in with current research on attention deficit disorders, and certainly one could say that perhaps a student never learned to read well *because* he had trouble paying attention—not the other way around. But even if this is true, too often children diagnosed as attention-deficit disordered are simply assumed to be incapable of becoming good readers, and no one really makes the effort to get them going. And if reading *does* develop the ability to concentrate—and I'm sure it does—it's an obvious thing to try.

I have a funny story about this. I used to have a student, call him Bob, who was terrorizing the school, failing most of his classes, and in general being a real concern. His mother, I understand, was semithreatening to demand a very expensive outside placement for her son.

So we had a meeting. It was during the last period, when I had a class, so a special ed. tutor was sent down to my room. The kids were just going to read, I told her. She could sit and relax. She was a little apprehensive because there, right in front of her, was Bob.

But Bob, a few months earlier, had fallen in love with the Xanth novels, by Piers Anthony. He hadn't been much of a reader before then, but he loved the Xanth books. When I let him read, he would sit absolutely still—this from a kid whose specialty was getting himself thrown out of classes for outrageous behavior. In fact, he was reading so much that he had earned an A minus in my class for the previous quarter.

So the special ed. meeting on Bob started. First the special ed. team chairman went over Bob's last report card. Bob had the A minus in English, a D in Biology—and he had failed everything else.

"Ah, can you explain this, Mary?" he asked me.

"He gave me his Visa card number," I said brightly. No one laughed. Okay. "He did a lot of reading," I explained.

No one thought this was particularly noteworthy. Back to the team chairman.

"Well," he said thoughtfully, after studying Bob's record a while longer, "I think we can assume he's ADD."

I had finished a graduate degree in learning disabilities

about seven years earlier, but already the terminology had bypassed me.

"ADD?" I said faintly.

"Attention deficit disorder," he explained kindly. "Bob can't pay attention."

"Come down to my room," I invited him. "I can guarantee you that he's been sitting motionless for the whole period, reading a book."

They looked at me unbelievingly, but luckily, at that moment, the bell rang, and the special ed. tutor returned. "Bob didn't move at all!" she informed the group. "He read the whole time!"

And Bob continued reading. By his last year in high school he was paying attention and passing all his classes. I like to think that Piers Anthony, and Ann Rice, and Stephen King, and all the other authors I read with him had as much to do with that as anything else. He's in college now, and the last time he stopped by to see me he told me he had a 2.0 average. "And I'm going to do better next term," he promised. And he probably will. Plus he told me he's reading all the time. He couldn't even remember all the titles he'd read in the last few months.

Not only does wide reading develop the ability to concentrate, I think it exposes students to such a broad range of experiences and ideas that they simply find discussions more interesting than their nonreading friends. They probably know a bit more about a given subject to begin with and so have an easier time processing new information. They have more ideas to add. They're quicker to see subtleties. They usually really enjoy class discussions, while their nonreading friends barely endure them, covertly checking the clock, again and again.

And, of course, the ability to concentrate on class discussions and lectures is almost as major a factor in student success as is reading itself.

Avid Readers Weather
Personal Problems Better

Outside of the inability to read well and concentrate, emotional problems are the next biggest block to student success. It's hard to pay attention to any academic subject when your mother has just been diagnosed with breast cancer, or your girlfriend is in the hospital because of a drug overdose.

It's certainly not an original insight to say that the teenage years are very difficult ones for many students. Family crises that younger kids can weather pretty well—illness, death, divorce, a sudden move—can almost sink a teenager. Teenagers lack the innocence and resilience of childhood, as well as the autonomy and self-confidence of adulthood. They're very vulnerable. And, ironically, during this vulnerable time, the pressure on students to perform very well in school is greatest. "You need to get into a good college," we tell them. "You need to develop good study habits. Oh, and while you're at it, you'd better play a sport. Maybe two sports. Get a job, too."

Avid, sophisticated readers who are going through a very difficult personal time have a much better chance of coming through it with their academic credentials intact than poor readers do. Avid readers can keep up with their work, using only a fraction of their emotional energy and time. Poor readers will often find that the great amounts of energy and time they need to keep up academically just aren't available to them during a time of crisis. So on top of their personal crises they usually experience much school failure as well, adding to their distress and low self-esteem.

Avid readers have another advantage. Their wide reading exposes them to a variety of opinions and life experiences. I've noticed that sometimes avid readers seem better able to bring some humor and perspective to their problems. Not always, of course, but sometimes. Teenagers whose sole exposure to life experiences other than their own comes from sitcoms and horror movies often lack the imagination or savvy to find creative solutions to problems. They're easily overwhelmed.

And, of course, avid readers, who are often good writers as well, can sometimes use their sophisticated literary ability to put some kind of shape on their problems. Sometimes if you can articulate the tragedies in your life, they don't have so much power over you. One sixteen-year-old boy, a wonderful, avid reader from a very troubled background, described his despair like this:

> *Sinbad, Gulliver, Dolittle, and oh, my mother*
> *please sing me a sea-farer's tune*
> *Wrap it up in close harmonies*
> *to stroke, then snag the blood-red moon.*
>
> *Jesus, sweet Lord Jesus,*
> *I've drowned and I'm cold*
> *I want your arms around me*
> *To keep me from shrinking and slowly slipping*
> *Now that I've grown old.*

Certainly, a habit of reading won't insulate your son or daughter from difficult teenage times—but I think it will help.

Avid Readers Have a Better Chance for a Successful, Fulfilling Adult Life

Teenagers are my area of expertise, not adults. However, just from my own experience, I see a number of ways avid reading makes adult life easier.

With the explosion of information in the workplace, only avid readers can stay relatively effortlessly well-informed. How can someone who can't quickly scan a report ever keep up with the volume of new theories and data?

Avid readers are also going to have an easier time writing reports and letters, and their writing will be much more literate and fluent than their mediocre-reading colleagues. Poorly written reports and manuals are a major problem for companies. Remember the early computer manuals? And companies aren't alone in this problem. Go to a library and browse through some professional journals. It's like wading through sludge. Who knows what valuable research is lost forever in awkward, jargon-laden sentences?

When faced with a new situation, avid readers tend to head for the library. I know that, when I was having my children, the volumes I read on pregnancy and child care helped make up for the fact that my own mother was hundreds of miles away. I didn't live near an extended family, but I had Ilg and Ames, and Dr. Spock, and Dr. Brazelton, and countless others to rely on. And when my older daughter was born with a cleft palate, I didn't panic. I was in graduate school at Brown University and so used my student ID to get access to the university medical library. It didn't matter that all the different navy pediatricians we saw often knew little about the management of a cleft palate child; I was up on the latest research.

I always feel very sorry for adults I see who are not readers. This summer I was called for jury duty. Jury duty, in Middlesex County in Massachusetts, consists of a lot of sitting in a jury pool room waiting to see if you'll be called. I had a new mystery to read, so I was perfectly happy waiting. I found a comfortable chair and curled up next to a window overlooking a courtyard filled with flowers. What a pleasant way to spend a morning.

My nonreading colleagues were not so happy. They paced the floor, made phone calls, leafed through magazines, and complained endlessly about having to wait. What did they do, I wondered, in dentists' waiting rooms, on airplanes, or in any situation where the television was not around?

And why do we have so many adults who aren't avid readers? We have adults who dislike reading, of course, because they were turned off to reading as children. In the next chapter I explain how this happens.

2

WHY SO MANY KIDS HATE READING

HOW BIG IS THE PROBLEM? IS YOUR SON OR DAUGHTER the only teenager in the country who hates reading?

A few facts you may know already: average verbal SAT scores had declined in 1991 to the lowest level in twenty years. Even the scores of our top students are declining. In 1972, 116,630 students scored above 600 on the verbal SAT; in 1991 this number was down to 74,000. During the same period the number of students scoring over 600 in math held steady—indicating that we are not seeing a drop in the intelligence or reasoning power of students, only in their verbal sophistication.

You'll be interested to hear the comments of Diane Ravitch, deputy U.S. Education Secretary and, according to the *Boston Globe,* a "well-known education researcher and writer." Ravitch is quoted in the *Globe* as saying, "There is too much TV, not enough reading; the results are confirming everything we know about kids' and parents' behavior. TV is written in short, declarative sentences."

I'm fascinated by her comment. She understands immediately, as I think most sensible people do, that kids score low on SATs because they don't read enough. But who is in charge of ensuring that children read? Their parents, who only see the kids when everyone's tired at night and everyone is loaded down with housework or homework? Or their teachers, who have them as a captive audience six hours a day, five days a week, for years—and who are supposedly the reading experts? Of course, it's the parents' fault—and the kids' fault.

During the summer of 1990, the National Assessment of Educational Progress, popularly known as the Nation's Report Card, said few students in grades four, eight, and twelve had actually mastered reading and writing. This isn't very surprising, because they found students reported doing very little reading. At all three grade levels, for example, 47 percent to 61 percent reported reading ten or fewer pages each day for schoolwork across the curriculum. The report, of course, blamed parents for not working enough with their children at home, and for allowing too much television watching.

I don't see that the question of *why* so many children and teenagers resist reading is part of the national discussion on reading failure. When it is raised at all, the answer is assumed: it's the parents' fault. If the children are little and not loving books, it's because the parents aren't reading enough bedtime stories. If the children are older, they hate reading because the parents allow them to watch too much television.

While I think it's undeniable that children raised in homes without books, and without parents who love reading, are at a great disadvantage, I think the disadvantage arises more because, often, a love of reading is *only* taught by parents. If children don't have parents who love to read, there is no one else to pass along this love, because schools don't seem to be in that business at all. In fact, schools are so successful in presenting reading as a distasteful chore that even children raised to love reading will sometimes learn to hate the sight of books before they ever reach junior high. From elementary school through high school, we do all we can to ensure that most kids would rather clean out a gerbil cage than curl up with a good book.

So why do so many kids hate reading? This is how I see it:

We Put Children in Ability Groups So We Can Teach Them Skills

Suppose, instead of kids just teaching themselves how to play video games, we decided that *we* had to teach them.

Okay, let's do it like this: First we put each child in front of a video screen, with a learning game on it, and tell him to do the simple moves this (boring) learning game requires. Oops. Johnny and Carrie can't push those buttons very fast. Plus they seem to get confused easily. Okay, let's separate them out, and put them in a remedial video game group. Five or six other kids are able to do the training game, but do it pretty slowly. They can go in the average video game group. The couple of kids who are pretty fast go into the accelerated group.

Okay, now we have them all grouped. We give each group special video training games to practice on. The remedial group gets a game that requires them to push the same button over and over again. This is so they can acquire the button-pushing skill. Of course it's boring and humiliating, but we don't want to give them something they can't do. The average group gets a game that's a little more interesting, to play over and over again, and the accelerated group maybe gets a real game.

I'm sure you get the picture. There's a good chance those children in the low video game group will grow to hate video games. They fail at them. They're segregated. The games they're given to play are only skill exercises, not really games at all. Even the average video group is not going to be thrilled with video games.

Of course you're seeing that this is exactly what most schools do with reading. A child who enters first grade and doesn't immediately and almost effortlessly pick up reading skills is forever marked a poor reader. He's put in low groups. He may even be removed from the classroom completely and put into a special ed resource room. He's given boring skill exercises to do. Any books he is given are usually basal readers that have been written to accommodate every special interest group in the country—every special interest group except children who don't like reading.

Contrast, for a minute, what happens with a child who doesn't acquire oral language as rapidly as his friends. Some children, by the age of eighteen months, are speaking in complete, short sentences. Other children don't acquire sentences until almost a whole year later.

How do we handle this? Do we segregate the children who are slow in speaking? Do we spend hours a day drilling them? ("Say *chair*. Now again!") Of course not. They play all the time with their more fluent friends, we talk to them all the time, and by the age of three or so they've caught up. By the time they're four no one even remembers which child started talking first.

There is an effort now, in a number of school districts, to try to avoid grouping children by ability as much as possible (more on this later), and to teach children to read by giving them regular trade children's books. It's called the whole language method, and if your school district is moving in this direction do all you can to encourage it. It's a wonderful approach because it recognizes that skills don't need to be discretely taught, one by one, but will be acquired if children simply fall in love with books and spend hours and hours poring over them. With a bit of initial help in figuring out words, these children have a chance of being wonderful readers.

Unfortunately, I've not yet gotten any graduates of the whole language method in my high school classroom. My classes still have far too many students who learned to read slowly, always felt like failures at reading, and so now avoid reading at all costs. It's possible to turn these students around, but it takes much time and effort.

And it's really incredible to me that it's only now, after *years* of grouping children and having them spend hours and hours doing boring, dumb things like phonics work sheets, and basal reader comprehension questions, that the educational specialists are finally saying, hey, maybe kids learn *how* to read by actually reading real *books!* And maybe it's not okay to continually make them do activities they completely dislike, and call these activities *reading.* And maybe, you know, telling kids they're dumb year after year by putting them in low-ability groups *may* have an effect on how they view reading!

Unbelievable.

Kids Are Encouraged to Read Only ''Good'' Literature

It's ironic, but just as our culture is producing more and more fairly mindless entertainment for kids—such as video games, violent movies, cable TV with whole channels devoted to rock videos—adult "experts" in children's literature seem to be demanding that children read only "good quality" literature. And actually, the literature needs not only to be good quality, it needs to be politically correct as well.

In a bid for a child's attention, a *Batman* comic might have a chance over a rock video—but a beautifully illustrated book on how the Hopi Indians planted corn probably isn't even in the running. Kids, after all, are kids, and actually enjoy such entertainment as reruns of Brady Bunch sitcoms. This is the clientele we are trying to reach.

Once when I was teaching in Norfolk, we decided to interview all of the incoming ninth-graders who had scored above the ninetieth percentile in reading. What did they read as kids, we asked them. Did they do a lot of reading? Every student but one reported reading some kind of serial or category fiction. The holdout was a black inner-city student, who tested in the ninety-fifth percentile. No, she didn't read Nancy Drew. She didn't read the Little House books. She didn't like romances, or fantasy, or mysteries.

How did she score so high? I didn't find out until a couple of weeks later, when another teacher came to me to complain because he had caught her reading comic books in his class.

"Aha!" I said to her. "That's what you read—comic books?"

She laughed and admitted it. "My brother and I have hundreds," she told me. "We collect them. I've read them for years."

I pay attention to what my excellent high school readers read as children, and I see the same thing again and again. They read huge amounts of junky subliterature. Often they get embarrassed when I ask them what they read—I'm an English teacher, after all—but when they finally realize that I'm not going to criticize them, they make long lists of Nancy Drew books, Sweet Valley books, comic books, fantasy series, war novels, Dr. Who books, and many other series I've never even heard of.

Now walk into the children's section of your local library. How many Dr. Who books do you see? How many Sweet Valley books? How many comic books?

You probably will find some Sweet Valley books, some Babysitter books, a few Nancy Drews and Hardy Boys, maybe a few Dr. Who books, but no comics. Why not more of the series books? Why not a whole wall full of comic books? I asked a librarian one time why she didn't stock comic books. She told me she couldn't because "the kids would just steal them."

At first I was angry at her answer, feeling that librarians just didn't care if kids read or not. But since then I've seen too many librarians who are saddened at how few older children are avid readers. Libraries are full of preschoolers and early elementary age kids happily browsing in the picture-book section. But older kids use the libraries mostly for school reports. And few librarians have the budget to really stock up on the kind of reading that would draw these older kids back.

Here's a suggestion: in many libraries adults pay a dollar or two to "rent" a best-seller that's just out. Perhaps children's librarians could acquire every title of the most popular series books, along with a large selection of comic books, and "rent" them out to children, or require a small deposit when kids check them out. I'm sure that most parents, who are continually shelling out two or three dollars to rent a video, would be delighted to rent books for their kids instead.

This would get kids regularly into libraries, and when their mania for series books finally pales, they would be in the habit of reading, used to going to libraries, and ready to move on to more complex literature.

I think this would help turn libraries from places where older kids go just to do reports to places full of older kids browsing, reading, and checking out books.

Of course, much more depressing than libraries, where librarians are at least *trying* to get kids to read, are classrooms and reading "labs." Although many elementary classrooms have little library sections (usually filled with "good" books), few junior high or high school classrooms are so stocked. Nothing is in sight but textbooks and workbooks. Any books that are on the shelves are almost always classics.

I'm not sure what's happening in publishing, but I know that I'm having a harder and harder time finding books with the lure of S. E. Hinton's early ones. I think the situation is this:

Publishers of children's books have two kinds of buyers:

children themselves, and adults who buy for children. Books written to be sold directly to children, mostly comics and series books, are just what kids want. Kids love these books. Books written to be filtered through children's book critics, and then sold to schools and libraries, are more often books that adults think children *should* love. And while we adults are pretty good at picking things (movies, books, toys, dolls, clothes) that our younger children will like, we lose that ability as the children grow older.

My guess is that thirty years ago publishers didn't worry so much about this second market of critics who recommend good children's books. They need to worry now, of course, because these critics are very powerful. A children's title that wins a Newbery or a Caldecott award will almost certainly be bought by almost every children's librarian, and featured in most bookstores. Publishers have a powerful economic incentive to please these critics.

To show you how far apart the taste of these critics and the taste of older children is, consider this. For the last couple of years, in the *Publishers Weekly* list of best-selling titles for middle-grade children, the Ann Martin Babysitter Club books have usually captured at least four out of the five places. The Babysitter Club books are very, very popular with elementary school kids. Now listen to this. In neither the *New York Times Parent's Guide to the Best Books for Children*, by Eden Ross Lipson (Times Books, 1991), nor the *American Library Association Best of the Best for Children*, edited by Denise Perry Donavin (American Library Association, 1992), is Ann Martin even *mentioned*. Her Babysitter Club books don't even get a footnote. It's as if they don't exist.

Actually, these two guides to the best children's books omit *all* of the popular children's series: no Hardy Boys, Nancy Drew, or Sweet Valley books. No comic books. No horror books by R. L. Stine. No Star Trek books. All of the really "bread and butter" reading books are omitted.

Publishers must be schizophrenic, trying to please both critics and children.

The sad thing is that these award-givers and critics really do mean well. But they haven't seen what I've seen over the last twenty years: thousands and thousands of high school kids who hate reading. I think many of these kids would have been literate, enthusiastic readers if they had been encouraged to read the series books and comics that kids can easily love.

The influence of these literary critics stretches everywhere. I'm very afraid that the promising "whole language" approach to teaching reading, which I described earlier, will be compromised by literary critics who feel they know best what is "appropriate" for children to learn to read with. I'm not very hopeful that *Richie Rich* comic books—the reading material that caused all three of my own children to fall in love with reading—will play a large part in the new curriculum.

Really, the arrogance of these arbiters of children's taste quite takes my breath away sometimes. I heard a literary critic of children's books remark one time that she wouldn't recommend any book for children that she didn't enjoy herself. Children are only supposed to like what she likes? Does she enjoy giggling on the phone for an hour to a girlfriend, recounting in endless detail what two boys in the lunchroom said to her? Is she tempted to engage in Indian hand-wrestling a friend while she's supposed to be listening to a math lecture? Why on earth does she think children should only read the kind of books she likes—when in every other area of life their likes and dislikes are so divergent?

If, by chance, your child has escaped all the negative consequences of skill exercises and low grouping in school, he can still learn to hate reading by coming into contact with a real literary snob.

Junior High and High School Reading Is Almost All Teacher Assigned

For the last few years, whenever I've taught American literature or British literature, I've given my classes a choice. They can either read, for homework, the short selections contained in our high school anthology, or they can choose books from a reading list and do significantly more reading. The first few weeks, if they take this option, they have to choose pre–twentieth century authors, and then early twentieth century authors. Only at the end of the course can they choose contemporary writers.

I've given this option to seven classes so far, a total of over 175 students, and I've only had *one* student out of this group express a wish to read the shorter anthology pieces. This year I'm asking my students for a little anonymous feedback every couple of weeks. They write me little notes, and I try to adjust the classes so they better benefit the students. A few of the students use the opportunity to make suggestions about classroom procedure, tests, etc., but a more typical comment is this: "So far, I have really enjoyed the class, especially the independent reading and writing. It gives me a chance to choose and figure out what I like to read instead of *having* to read something I don't want to."

I could never assign the amount of reading that students do when they have a choice. I've had students average a book a week—books like *The Scarlet Letter* by Hawthorne, and *East of Eden* by Steinbeck. The chance that a student will enjoy a book doubles or triples when a student chooses that book himself.

When a student is assigned a book, the teacher—or curriculum committee, or department chairman, or school board, or state agency—is sending the message that the student's likes and dislikes are not important. It's not important if the student likes the book. He'd just better read it! For a student with low self-esteem to begin with—and most poor readers have low self-esteem because of all the school failure—this just reiterates what he already suspects about himself. He's worthless, and his taste in reading is worthless. Reading is certainly something he'd better stay away from.

Virtually all reading in junior and senior English classes is assigned. It's one reason, of course, that schools are holding so tenaciously to tracking. Tracking is the high school equivalent of grade school reading groups. Only in high school, kids are grouped into separate classes. There are, usually, honors classes, enriched classes, average classes, and basic classes. Later I'll discuss in some depth the effects of tracking, but tracking is important to note here because it is a necessary precondition for teachers to insist that all students in the class read the same book. To do that, the teacher needs to have students who have approximately the same reading level. Of course then the teacher can not only make all the students read the same books, she can make them do all the other things that make reading so distasteful to students: she can quiz every day, assign comprehension questions, assign vocabulary words, make the students do endless reports on theme, characters, setting, etc.

My feeling about this is that it doesn't hurt a literate, avid reader to learn how to analyze fiction—but when kids who don't like to read in the first place are turned off even more by a teacher who insists on endless analyzing, there's something wrong. It's almost as if the teacher is saying: "You don't like to read? Fine. I'm going to make sure that when you're through with my class you're not just going to mildly dislike reading, you're going to *hate* it!"

The notion that students should be able to choose much, or all, of their reading material is seen as hopelessly radical. Teachers are afraid that students really won't read. How can teachers check on them? (Actually, there's a greater chance that students will read if they choose their books. For one thing, they can't copy quiz answers off a friend, as they can when everyone is reading the same book.)

I think control, and basic distrust of kids, is an issue here too. Most educators, for all their talk about respecting human differences and helping the individual child, really don't think children—or certainly teenagers—can play any important role in their own education. Maybe kids will choose "inappropriate" books! Censorship is always lurking around the corner in any curriculum discussion.

I am always amazed that, in the current controversies over what kind of reading should be assigned to college students—whether they should read Western, classic authors, or more of a mix of minority and Third World authors—no one ever suggests that the students be given a reading list and choose their own books. They could share their findings with each other. Rather than a whole class period spent discussing one book, students could report on a multitude of books and everyone's knowledge would be greatly expanded. In my classes, students read many books independently, and a few books together with their classmates. The books they read together give everyone a common reference for discussion, and the books read independently really enrich the discussions.

But no. Everyone in a class reads only the same books. And even students who actually enjoyed reading as children stand a good chance of learning to hate reading as teenagers.

Students Don't Read Well Enough to Enjoy Reading

Many students, and parents, and teachers, don't understand that at the heart of many students' dislike of reading is often an inability to read fluently.

We expect the students whom we know have reading problems to dislike reading—students who have been diagnosed as learning disabled, or who have a history of learning how to read very late. But why do students who initially learned to read very easily also often hate reading?

I think what happens is this. Because of all of the early emphasis on skill development, no one particularly worries when these facile readers decide to spend much of their free time playing soccer, or ice-skating, or just hanging around playing video games. They have the skills. They're testing at or above grade level. Skill development, and not avid-reading behavior, is the goal everyone is looking at. So when other students start reading independently in third or fourth grade, these students don't.

But because these students do not read for pleasure, they gradually lose their edge in reading. They never gain the fluency and sophistication of their avid-reading peers. As a result, every year they fall further and further behind. While the children's books they used to read were easy for them, the books they are expected to read in junior high and high school are very difficult. They get confused by multiple plots and characters. They miss subtleties of style and theme. It takes them a long time to do the assigned reading at night.

Naturally, they assume that they dislike reading. Since they do only assigned reading, and assigned reading has become too hard for them, they figure that they just dislike reading in general. They *used* to read well, relatively speaking, so they assume that they still do. It's just that all books have lately gotten boring.

Actually, they are not alone in not realizing how weak they are in reading. Most students who read poorly have no idea how much easier it is for a good reader to read the same book they're struggling with. When an avid reader in my class will casually remark that he read a whole book over the course of a day or two, my poor readers initially don't believe him. "Yeah, right," they say. "You read the back of the book." Either that, or they assume the avid reader is a complete nerd who does *nothing* all day except read. How else could he finish a book so quickly?

You can compare the view of reading of a poor reader with the view of the world of a person who needs glasses but doesn't have them. Neither knows what he is missing. The first time I put glasses on I was astonished to see the world as everyone else saw it. I never realized objects had crisp, clear edges, and that one could easily recognize friends across a street. Similarly, a poor reader doesn't realize how easily and effortlessly an avid reader goes through a book.

Of course, conscientious poor readers often have the hardest time of all. They spend so much time trying to understand the reading assigned in their classes that they have no time to pick up easier, more enjoyable reading, if they were ever so inclined. As they progress through high school and college, reading gets harder and harder since the books get more difficult, and the amount of reading skyrockets. They're in a no-win situation. They read so slowly that the only kind of reading they have time for is the difficult, assigned reading that probably won't do much to help their reading skills. The assigned reading certainly won't help them learn to love books, and you can be sure that when they do have a little free time they won't use it trudging to the nearest library or bookstore.

There is Not a Critical Mass of Readers Among Young People

When I grew up, in the 1950s, all of my friends loved to read. We traded *Batman* and *Little Lulu* comic books; we lent each other our new Nancy Drew mysteries; we passed around forbidden copies of *Catcher in the Rye* and giggled over the profanity.

While some late elementary school and junior high girls

still do this with the Babysitter and Sweet Valley books, I
see very little of this behavior with my high school students.
The avid readers are few and far between, and usually they
are reluctant to share their latest, wonderful reading discovery because their classmates will think they're a little odd.
Books are not something that one should get excited about.

It's possible in a classroom, however, to nurture this kind
of book sharing. In most of my classes I take a day every
week or two to hear about everyone's independent reading.
The main purpose, of course, is to have students hearing
other students recommend books. As the semester goes on,
certain books will sweep the class. *East of Eden* swept my
American literature class two years ago, and *Go Ask Alice*
swept one of my sophomore classes. Robert Parker's Spenser books will often sweep, as will certain Stephen King
titles.

When families were bigger, I think this "critical mass" of
readers would often happen among brothers and sisters.
When I taught in a Catholic school in Virginia, around 1978,
I happened to ask my accelerated ninth-grade class to list
the names of their brothers and sisters. Hands went up. "All
of them?" a number of kids asked. "Yes, all," I told them.
Well, in this class of excellent readers I had only *one* only
child, and no one from a family of just two children. The
entire rest of the class, about twenty-five kids, were from
families of three or more children. Some had ten or eleven
siblings. Most tended to be one of the younger ones in the
family. They were the tail end of the huge Catholic families
of the fifties and sixties.

And they grew up surrounded not only by the comics and
series books of their many older brothers and sisters, they
had the brothers and sisters themselves around to offer advice about interesting reading material. Just for fun, I asked
my lower-level class the same question about the numbers
of brothers and sisters. I can't remember their exact num-

bers, but I do remember that they were from significantly smaller families.

Librarians, parents, and teachers have taken over the job of recommending books to children, and unfortunately, we don't do nearly as good a job as friends and siblings used to do.

I have a good story that shows the power of a friend recommending a book. A few years ago I agreed to take over the Alternative Program in English for a few weeks. The students in this program, for various reasons, had not been able to perform very well in mainstream classes. One of the students, I knew, was an extremely poor reader. He was also famous for being hostile and uncooperative. Luckily, another student in that program was a good friend of both of ours. I talked privately to this other student and pointed out that his friend was a very poor reader. "He absolutely *needs* to read," I told him, "and I think the only book he has much of a chance of getting through is S. E. Hinton's *That Was Then, This Is Now.*"

Our mutual friend shrugged, but when I walked into the Alternative Program classroom and spilled a large number of paperbacks on a table for the students to choose from, he picked up the S. E. Hinton book and tossed it to his friend. "Read this!" he commanded, and his friend obediently picked up the book and sat down to read. It took the poor reader about two weeks to get through that book, but then he was on his way. I later had this poor reader in a couple of my mainstream classes, and he gradually read more and more—though he always checked with that first friend for help in choosing books, never with me!

So now you have an idea of why your child may be turned off to reading. But what do you do about it? Can you just find that perfect school?

3

WHAT TO DO

IN THE LAST CHAPTER, I DETAILED MANY THINGS THE schools do to make reading a chore rather than a joy. What kind of schools *would* be sure to turn out avid readers? Here is my dream of the perfect school.

Elementary School

Every classroom in this school would be flooded with kid-friendly reading material. There would be piles of *Richie Rich* comics on the counters, the bookcases would be jammed with Babysitter books and Hardy Boys mysteries, beanbag chairs and pillows and couches would be scattered around the room in comfortable reading corners, and the classroom would be run by a teacher who was an avid reader herself. During each school day the kids would be given two or three hours to read any material of their choice. No tests. While they read the teacher could read herself, part of the time, and work with individuals or groups on math, science, writing, or reading projects the rest of the time. As the children became more sophisticated readers, the teacher could gently branch them out to many of the wonderful nonfiction children's books being written today on a wide variety of subject matter. The children would not only end up as excellent readers, they would have acquired a depth of knowledge in various subjects that they don't begin to get currently from their watered-down, boring textbooks.

I can just hear elementary teachers saying, "The children would never sit still and read for that amount of time." But I think that if the reading material were interesting enough to them, they would. They won't sit still for three hours and read a basal reader, but they will sit still for *Batman* comics and Dr. Who books. I know that elementary teachers will also say that they have too much else they need to do; there's no time in the schedule for two or three hours of reading a day. I say, change the schedule. Nothing is more important.

Junior High and High School

Again, I would like to see in every classroom piles of reading material: paperback fiction in English classrooms; newspapers, news magazines, historical fiction and nonfiction in social studies classrooms; science magazines and good, interesting trade science paperbacks (like Carl Sagan's writing) in science classrooms; foreign language magazines, comics, and easy fiction in foreign language classrooms. And math? This is really out of my field, but I know some math teachers do wonderful things with games, and I imagine there are magazines and books that support this more inductive approach to math.

And I can hear secondary teachers saying, just like their elementary school colleagues, that there is no time in the curriculum for this kind of independent reading. And again I say, I think we need to change the curriculum. High-interest, student-chosen, independent reading should be a major part of every course.

What Are the Chances of Your Finding Schools Like These for Your Kids?

You have zero chance.

Why?

Education is moving in the opposite direction. Listen to the policy makers both on your local and national level. The buzzwords are *accountability, national curriculum, high standards.* Now I ask you: Will this translate into children being able to spend two or three hours a day in school reading Nancy Drew mysteries? Don't hold your breath.

The other major drag on kids ever falling in love with reading comes from our universities. We have all sorts of reading professionals up there, who publish (so they don't perish, presumably) countless studies on what discrete reading skills children have or don't have. They study children as one would study vacuum cleaners or ketchup bottles. They don't really talk to the children; they don't ask them why they read or why they don't read. They don't ask them what books they like. They certainly don't ask them how their teacher might manage things in the classroom to help them enjoy reading more.

No, they test their vocabulary, word recognition, spelling, and comprehension skills—their comprehension of short paragraphs, mind. At least that's what Jeanne S. Chall, a professor of education at Harvard University, Vicki A. Jacobs, the assistant director of teacher education at Harvard University, and Luke E. Baldwin, associate professor of education at Lesley College did. In their book, *The Reading Crisis: Why Poor Children Fall Behind* (Cambridge, Massachusetts: Harvard University Press, 1990), they follow a group of about thirty lower-income children up until the eleventh grade. They find that, although these children test on grade level up until the third grade, they start falling behind after that. By the eleventh grade they are far behind in reading. Their recommendation to the schools: do more of the same (use basal readers, teach vocabulary, use some regular children's books for enrichment, etc.) but do it better. This doesn't make any sense to me. The status quo isn't working at all. (Yet it's interesting to see, isn't it, that the children apparently enter school, at age six, pretty well prepared. The longer the schools have these kids, the worse the kids do.) But these researchers pull out the magic words like *structure* and *skill development* and two of them are, after all, professors from Harvard University. They have a very powerful influence on the teaching of reading. And, to be fair, it's hard to imagine what a recommendation like mine—that children be given whatever they want to read, including comics and series fiction, for two or three hours every day—would do for the professors' careers. I just wish that somewhere, in their book, one could hear the voices of the children they tested. What was the children's *experience* of school reading? How did they get to eleventh grade, reading so poorly? But the feeling and opinions of children have never been part of the national discussion on reading. It certainly isn't part of the endless research all the "experts" cite.

The third reason you won't find any schools like the ones I recommend is that few elementary and secondary teachers are avid readers themselves. The December 1991 *Wall Street Journal* reported that college freshmen who planned to teach scored an average of 847 total points on the Scholastic Aptitude Test. The highest possible score is 1600 points, 800 on the verbal section and 800 on the math. Since most people score slightly higher on the math section, we can guess that the average verbal score was around 420. Now remember, this was the *average* score. A good number of the prospective teachers must have scored *below* this.

I don't think I've seen an avid reader score below the high 500s on the verbal section of the SAT. Most score well into the 600s or 700s. This means that the vast majority of teachers have never experienced the excitement and wonder of being totally absorbed in book after book after book. No wonder they think basal readers, workbooks, and vocabulary drill are perfectly appropriate ways of teaching reading.

So where does this leave us? We have college professors who make brief forays into elementary and secondary classrooms, administer a few tests, and then decide they know what's going on, and we have teachers who are indifferent readers themselves.

This leaves us in the position of not being able to count on the schools to develop a love of reading in our children. If you're lucky, you may find pockets of reading-loving teachers in reading-friendly schools. Although I've never heard of any that go to the lengths I suggest in the beginning of this chapter, certainly there are teachers who love books and manage to pass that love on to their students. My impression is that they're a little more prevalent in elementary schools; the higher up the education ladder your children travel, the less likely they are to find reading-loving teachers. And you can never *count* on your children having teachers who try to help them love reading. So you need to be prepared to develop that love yourself.

How to Develop a Love of Reading in Children

That's what the rest of this book is about. I'll suggest a game plan to help you keep your goal firmly in mind. I'll identify the stages I've watched hundreds of readers progress through. I'll suggest ways for you to run a reading-friendly house. I'll give some thoughts on managing television. And, finally, I'll include a rather extensive section on coping with the schools that are available to us now. I don't think we can easily change the direction of education in this country, but I do firmly believe that we can enable our own children, at least, to love reading.

4

GAME PLAN

YOUR MAJOR GOAL IS CLEAR: YOU WANT YOUR CHILDREN to love reading so they'll spend plenty of time reading and so become wonderful readers. Unfortunately, as I've explained in the second chapter, much of your children's school experience will *not* help them love reading. In addition, as you already know, our culture today doesn't do much to support reading. Our kids today seem completely taken up with video games, after-school sports, skiing lessons, and hundreds of other activities. Your children probably have few friends who spend a lot of time reading. A love of reading, for our children today, doesn't just happen. This chapter is about how to make it happen.

Take the Long View

I think it's good to be clear about goals. You want your child to love reading. That's your major goal. Your major goal isn't to get your son into the top reading group in elementary school, or your daughter into Harvard with a verbal SAT score of 750. Harvard would be great (and expensive). But if you make a specific accomplishment like this your major goal, you risk losing everything. Let me explain.

My younger daughter fell in love with playing the clarinet. This was pure serendipity: except for a little piano playing on her father's and my part, no one else in our family ever played a musical instrument. And it turned out she had talent. She was in her school orchestra, then she tried out for stage band and made it, then she tried out for the junior district band and made it.

Then she told me she was tired of stage band and wanted to quit.

The teacher in me was thinking: she should take this music all the way. It might be a ticket to college. (Colleges, I knew, don't want a well-rounded person, they want a well-rounded *school*. They like experts in various fields, but the experts themselves don't have to be well-rounded.)

But luckily, my common sense took over and I thought: what's my goal? I would like her to keep her love of music. I would like music to be a pleasure in her life. If I force her to stay in stage band, and she's not enjoying it, her love and enthusiasm for playing will probably decrease.

So we talked about her concerns about stage band, and I told her that she could certainly quit if she wanted to. It was her decision. So far she hasn't quit, but I fully expect her to. And that's okay. I want her to enjoy music. It's hard to enjoy doing something if someone is holding a gun to your head.

How does this work with reading?

Simply, you don't want to do anything that will make reading seem like a chore. It's better to have your son do just a little bit of reading at home at first—he'll read more later, trust me—than to have him read a lot but only when you're forcing him.

Now I understand that many people believe that few activities are fun until we develop our skills at them through necessary drill and practice. I don't believe this myself, but it is an argument. But just remember that your child is already being forced to do much nonfun drill and practice work in reading at school. You don't want to add to the burden. It's very important that the reading you entice your child into is pleasurable. Remember, you're taking the long view.

Ask yourself, what is more important? Is it more important that your daughter be in all honors English classes in high school or that she become a lifelong reader? If you force her to read, you may get her reading level up to a point where she can excel in school, but she may become so turned off to reading that she never opens another book. I've had kids in class who have been forced to read when they were younger. They always read only what is required. Nothing more.

You want your daughter to *love* reading, so that it's always there, as a source of strength and joy in her life. If she loves reading, she'll keep getting better and better as a reader. And her world will keep expanding: she'll stay open to new ideas, new information. In a real sense, she'll stay young.

Your child is already at risk of never achieving this love because of much of what is going on in the schools. You can't afford to add to the risk.

So what can you do? Think, for a minute, of the activities you really enjoy. I suggest that they have these common elements: you're good at them, they provide a sense of accomplishment, and you get totally engrossed in them and manage to temporarily shut out the world and its problems.

How does this translate to reading?

Provide Reading Material That Is Easy and Fun for Children

This would seem like an obvious rule, but it isn't. Believe me, it isn't. Somehow, in our culture, we think that unless something is hard for us to do, it isn't worthwhile. And when children are always being given something hard to do, when they are always struggling, they lose their sense of competence. They don't feel good at this activity. So they don't like it.

Suppose you only played tennis against players who were much better than you. I can guarantee you that, after a while, it wouldn't be fun anymore. It's no fun always to lose.

Children don't think it's fun to be always struggling through books they have trouble understanding. And we teachers are notorious for always giving students books they'll have trouble with. It keeps us in control, as the teacher-who-knows-everything. What's the point of giving a student a novel he can read without our help? He might as well read it on his own at home. (Of course, he *doesn't* read it on his own at home—but that's the parent's fault, right? Ha!)

So you, as the parent, have to give your children books they can easily and readily enjoy. Many well-meaning parents don't understand this. A couple of years ago I had a student who was lukewarm at best toward reading. Books didn't interest him. Reading was boring.

After a while I gave him *Misery*, by Stephen King. Instant hit! He loved it! And he regaled the class every day with the episodes from the book he had read the night before. The writer was caught. The lady was torturing him. She cut off his feet! The class was all ears, and this young gentleman was having the time of his life. Then he finished the book, and when I tried to give him another Stephen King, he sadly shook his head. His mother had gotten a book for him. I can't remember which one it was—something about an Indian and forests—but it was a recognized classic, and she didn't want him reading any more "trash."

He dutifully plowed through it, but at a much slower pace than he had read *Misery*, and without the glee. Plus his descriptions of this book bored the class—I think they bored him. It wasn't a happy experience for him, or us, and when I tried to explain this to his parents on conference day I quickly saw it was a lost cause. His father wandered over to the bookshelves in my room, scanned the authors' names (Danielle Steel, Robert Ludlum, V. C. Andrews, lots of Stephen King), and sniffed, "Drugstore books."

"Excuse me?" I asked.

"These are books you see in a drugstore. You don't have any good books here."

He just didn't understand that these "drugstore books" were the key for his son to acquire a love of reading.

Actually, by high school age, many students themselves have also acquired the sense that they shouldn't read "easy" books. I used to leave some teenage romances on my shelves—they're wonderful for girls who are slow readers—but I finally had to hide them under the shelves because so many of the students would see them and proclaim loudly that they had read these books in elementary school and junior high. They said these books were too easy! This ruined the books for the students who really needed this fun, easy reading experience. Now I try to slip the romances out and into the hands of these students without anyone else seeing.

I think what is really sad is when students themselves feel that, if they can quickly and enjoyably read a book, they shouldn't. I have students who are afraid to read books they think are too easy. They are never students who are excellent readers. Excellent readers are used to breezing through books. It's one reason they love reading. They're so good at it! They can do it effortlessly!

You want to duplicate this experience for your mediocre or poor readers. You want them to have the experience of effortlessly breezing through books. So fast, easy-reading books are worth their weight in gold. Look for them. Encourage your children to read them. They'll move on after a while. Books that are too easy will become boring to them. But let that happen naturally. Don't try to rush it. Allow your children to read books that make them feel like wonderful readers.

Increase Your Child's Self-Confidence by Treating Him as a Reading Expert in His Field

It is a pretty well kept secret that children *want* to be good readers. They feel good about being able to read. I never hear my avid-reading high school students taunted for being bookworms. They're admired.

It's a real turning point when a student starts to see himself as a reader. It's a major change in his self-image. You can help this out by taking his interests seriously, and by always assuming that of course he likes to read. Maybe he just hasn't found the right books yet. No one likes to read everything.

Ask your son's opinion about the books he's reading. Take his opinion seriously. Recognize him as an expert, even if it's just in Choose Your Own Adventure books. Always treat him as a reader, and sooner or later he'll be one.

A high point in my teaching career came when a student of mine, whom I helped to get reading, was describing a friend of his whom I didn't know. "He's a reader like I am," he explained seriously, and I felt a glow warm me through. He certainly was a reader—still is, as a matter of fact. But five years ago being a reader was not part of his self-image. Now it is.

If you have a preschooler, you can start this very early. Ask his opinion: which are the best Richard Scarry books? Recognize his expertise on Dr. Seuss. Have grave discussions on the relative merits of the Berenstain Bears books. At an early age make it clear that you value his opinion as a literary person.

The worst thing you can do is to ignore the tastes of your children. That tells them that they're not important, that their tastes don't matter. Then reading isn't something that will enhance their self-esteem. If you denigrate their choices you make them feel bad about their choices—and about themselves—and about reading.

A student I once had moved on to another teacher who allowed no choice in books. He came back to see me. "She doesn't *know* that I like S. E. Hinton and basketball books," he said sadly to me. "She just shoves a book at me and says to read it."

"Maybe the book she gave you will be good," I said brightly, but he just shook his head. The point for him wasn't whether the book she gave him was a good book or not; the point was that he had started seeing himself as a reader with definite tastes, but she didn't recognize that. He wasn't a reader to her, just another student.

So don't make that mistake with your children. Treat them as serious readers, and reading will then be an activity that gives them a feeling of satisfaction. It will increase their self-esteem. They'll love reading. They'll read more!

Besides finding books that your children can read easily, and besides treating them seriously as readers, you need to keep one more thing in mind. We like activities that we can become completely absorbed in.

Find Books That Completely Absorb Your Children

As a teacher, this is the one aspect of reading that I find the most fun. I love to watch students become completely lost in a book. Last semester I had a student who informed me at the beginning of the year that he hated reading. He had *never* read a book that he enjoyed. Wow! What a challenge! It took me several months, but I finally thought to hand him a novel from the Brotherhood of War series. He was instantly hooked, and my fondest memory of him is watching him sit hunched over the book while the rest of the class filed out to lunch one day. He was so engrossed in the story that he hadn't even noticed that it was lunch-time—something a teenage boy rarely overlooks.

Of course, watching children being completely engrossed in something is one of the great joys of parenthood. I can still see my oldest daughter, at the age of three-and-a-half, parading through navy housing in her Halloween Cookie Monster costume. Navy housing was full of kids ("Midget Village" my friend called it), and so the streets were full of little witches and skeletons and other assorted creatures. "Hi, Bunny!" she'd say delightedly when she'd see some-one in a rabbit costume. "Hi, Witch! Hi, Pumpkin!" She was completely engrossed in this world. These other kids *were* witches and pumpkins and skeletons to her at that mo-ment. The fantasy was real for her.

In fact, this fantasy was so real that she wore her costume for months. In July she was trudging through the streets of Monterey with me in her blue furry outfit. The Cookie Monster, right in Monterey!

We want to find *books* that are this real for our children. And I don't think that we should worry that our children will be stuck in these fantasy worlds and never move on to more serious literature. A sad part of getting older, for me, is that so many fiction books don't work for me any-more. I can't get lost in them. I can see so clearly where the plot is going that I'm quickly bored. Stephen King, V. C. Andrews, Danielle Steel—the authors that my stu-dents love don't hold me. I find myself racing through, skipping large chunks, just trying to get the plot straight so I can enthusiastically assure my kids that I've read the books too.

It's a real find for me now to discover a writer who exerts that grip on me. Agatha Christie used to do it—although I think mainly I liked the upper-class English world of her books. With a husband at sea, and two small children to get off to day-care so I could go to work, I loved reading about the life-style of the characters in her books. Servants brought in morning tea and opened the drapes. The lady of the house sat up in bed, ate her breakfast, and read the morning mail. That's the life I wanted! The books completely absorbed me.

Actually, the "world" of books is often what captures children as well. They want to live in a fantasy world, with dragons and magic—or an old-fashioned world. Certainly I think my kids so loved the *Richie Rich* comic books because they wanted to live in such an outrageously rich world. When I had to tell them that, unfortunately, we couldn't afford to buy a horse ranch, they could escape to Richie's world and become absorbed in his private jets and mansions and diamonds.

I'll offer suggestions later on for books that I've found to be absorbing for different kinds of readers. But here it's just important to get the principle straight: help your children find books that will absorb them.

I think if you keep these three principles firmly in mind—easy books, absorbing books, your child as a reading expert—your child will start to thaw toward reading. Maybe not by junior high or high school, but surely by the time he's an adult, he'll start to love reading.

Some problems along the way:

If My Child Reads All These Trashy, Absorbing Books, Won't His Behavior Go Downhill?

This is a real concern for many parents, and certainly an understandable one. Obviously, if your choice is to have a son who hates reading but leads a solid, upstanding life as a banker—or an avid-reading son who is incarcerated for life in a prison for criminal deviates—you're going to choose having the banker. I would too. But I don't think the situation is that simple. The question is, how do books influence behavior?

A few observations first. All studies of incarcerated felons indicate that their average reading level is very low, usually somewhere around a fourth-grade level. Prisons are not full of avid readers. My own guess is that the less kids read, the more likely they will be unable or unwilling to adhere to society's standards and function as good citizens. The poor reader has experienced much less success in school and undoubtedly much more frustration in the job market. A poor reader is at much *higher* risk for criminal behavior.

But I don't think we usually worry that our child will go out robbing gas stations and mugging old ladies. We worry about more ordinary things. If our kids read enough Danielle Steel books, will they think you need to have a glamorous, rich life to be happy? Will they have nightmares after reading Stephen King? Will *Forever* by Judy Blume convince them that having sex at sixteen is fine? Will they read *Go Ask Alice* and decide to experiment with drugs?

I guess I have a very pragmatic attitude toward these worries. Face it: unless you manage to keep your children in a cocoon, they're going to be exposed to all of these ideas and influences anyway. They'll watch movies scarier than any book could possibly be. Almost all television sitcoms seemed imbued with the philosophy that a rich life-style is better. Sex? Sex in books is tame compared to sex in movies and on television. My theory is that kids might as well pick up reading skills rather than just video-watching skills.

Plus, I think wide, wide reading is the safeguard against our children simplistically "buying into" one book. If you've only ever lived in one town, on one street, in one house, your whole frame of reference is that town. That's reality to you. If people in that town are mean and cold and never help each other out, you're going to have a jaded view of humanity. But if you move around you see that people live in various ways; your sense of what constitutes reality is much broader. Maybe you see other towns where people are friendly and helpful.

That's why you want your children to be avid readers. It's like living in hundreds of towns all around the world. They read one book that seems to indicate that money helps people to be happy, but the next book they read will probably show wealth causing great unhappiness. Actually, *most* books your kids pick up will have philosophical outlooks you'll probably find compatible with yours. *Go Ask Alice* is about drugs, but most kids tell me, after reading it, that it makes them determined never to get involved with drugs. *Forever* does not end very happily for the teenager who has sex.

But the real safeguard is simply that your kids are reading so much that they should end up with a fairly balanced view of life. And even literature that is frankly escapist—fantasy novels, teenage romances—gives them a nice little break from their real-life problems. We can all use a break now and then. And what better break than reading? Surely you would rather have your son escape having to think about not making the track team for a while by reading a fantasy novel than by meeting some friends behind the closed auto shop and breaking out a six-pack?

Of course, it's tempting to think that you can have it all. You can have an avid reader who avidly reads only good books. Maybe this is possible; I've just never met a kid like this. I find that the minute parents (or teachers—we're experts at this) get too intrusive, picking out this book for a child, withholding that other book, the fun goes out of it for the kid. A big part of the fun of reading is picking your own books—and sometimes picking out books that maybe seem a little wicked . . . books that maybe your parents wouldn't approve of. . . .

I've always liked my mother's solution to the problem of trashy reading. Sometimes she'd notice some book that had me completely enthralled and say thoughtfully, "Maybe you shouldn't be reading that." Then she'd brighten and decide, "Well, if you shouldn't be reading it, you probably won't understand it anyway." And the funny thing was, she was right. I can vividly remember reading *The Scarlet Letter* and having no idea what the *A* embroidered on Hester's breast stood for. Kissing didn't start with *A* and that was about as far as my sexual knowledge went at the age of ten.

And I have to say that, in twenty years of teaching, I have never seen students who got caught by all the problems we parents have nightmares about—promiscuity, drug use, massive academic failure—because of books they've read. Personal trauma, family dysfunction: these are the kinds of unhappy situations that lead to self-destructive teenage behavior. If anything, as I mentioned earlier, a love of reading provides a little buffer. Avid readers can keep their grades up and bring more perspective to their tragedies.

And there is another interesting aspect to this trashy reading issue. I've found that most kids do a lot of self-censoring. My younger daughter, for example, refuses to read books about ghosts. She doesn't like being scared. I have kids who tell me they don't want to read depressing books. They like happy endings. Every so often, when I'm teaching *Catch-22*, a student will tell me he finds the book offensive. Fine. We find another book for that student. What kids instinctively know, and what children's literary critics seem unable to understand, is that the view of life in most so-called trashy books is usually more positive and upbeat than the view of life in most classics. Robert Cormier is considered one of the best writers of young adult novels (by the critics), but I find his view of life so bleak that I hate to submerge myself in it. And most of my students feel the same way. So while your child may make brief forays into books you'd just as soon he'd stay out of, he'll probably work his way back to books that have a life view more compatible with yours. And then he'll truly believe in that life view, because he's seen other sides.

So try to be casual about your child's reading. I've had

the sweetest young girls read literally hundreds of bodice-ripper romances. I've had the most realistic, sensible young men read hundreds of sword-and-dragon romances. Their reading hasn't changed these kids at all—except to make them more literate and to give them a better sense of humor. It probably all comes down to trusting your child, trusting that his, or her, innate good sense, and wonderful upbringing, will enable him or her to emerge from reading *anything* with just more wonder and understanding of our incredibly complex, mystifying human condition.

So please, don't censor. Trust your children!

But what if you've done all this? You've encouraged your son to read easy, engaging books, you treat him seriously as a reader, you don't censor—and he still spends very little time reading. Don't get upset yet. Other things come into play.

Some Kids Are Very Slow to Catch On to Reading

There are many reasons why some children don't pick up reading skills very easily. Some kids have a specific learning disability that makes reading harder. Some kids have an attention deficit disorder and have trouble concentrating. Some are just immature, and have trouble settling down to learn anything. If your child has a specific problem, it's important, of course, to get help for him. But it's also important to communicate to him that he *can* learn to read; it just might take him a little longer.

I'm very concerned with the impact a learning disability diagnosis, or a diagnosis of Attention Deficit Disorder, sometimes has on a child. I've had students say things like, "I'll never read well; I'm dyslexic." Except in a tiny percentage of cases, that doesn't need to be true. Kids acquire coping strategies as they get older. They may need more practice to read well, and they may never be able to spell, but most kids *can* be good readers.

If you have a child who is not picking up reading easily, it's even more important for you to find engrossing, easy books for him, and to treat him seriously as a reader. The *last* thing you want to do is to tell him that he is damaged in some way and can never read well. He can read well; believe me, he can. He just has to do lots and lots of reading. Later in this book I go into great detail about how to get poor readers started reading, but now you need to know that, although there is no magic bullet for teaching learning-disabled kids to read—I wouldn't waste too much time looking for that perfect school with that perfect teacher— your child *can* learn to read, and even more importantly, he can learn to *love* reading. Be enthusiastic. Be positive. Keep telling him that, no matter what stage he's at, he's doing *great*.

Sometimes kids don't seem to have any real trouble learning how to read, they just have other interests. It's important for parents to realize that some children, just because of the way they are, are never going to be bookworms. The very athletic child is probably the most obvious example.

Kids' Level of Activity Has Much to Do with How Much Reading They Do

My older daughter enjoys reading very much—almost as much as she enjoys playing soccer. I, who grew up knowing so little about sports that I just dimly recognized that balls were round, have a daughter with the balance, coordination, timing, and speed of a cat. She grew up walking on railings, two stories off the ground. She climbed to the very top of two-hundred-year-old trees. She could outrun every boy in the neighborhood.

Not only that, but her level of activity was always very

high. She likes to move. She was always up and out the door.

Now, it's hard to read when you're flying down the street to catch frogs or build rafts. Many kids are so active that it's difficult to get them to sit down and do *anything*. But there are some things you can do.

Realize that children like this will never be bookworms— at least probably not in your lifetime. My daughter did significantly less reading than I did when I was growing up— I was just a much more sedentary child—but she did do enough reading to be an excellent reader, and reading is still an activity that she really enjoys. I'm sure that as she gets older and starts to slow down a bit, she'll read even more. Because reading is a pleasure for her. She's always looking for the next good book. When she got her own apartment in Dover, New Hampshire, one of the first things she did was to get a library card from the Dover library.

So recognize when you have a child like this. She isn't going to sit around all day reading unless you tie her down with very strong rope—and then what will happen to her love of reading? Just tell yourself that she's nice and healthy from all that exercise, when she isn't getting stitched up from some mishap in the emergency room, and that as long as she *loves* reading, sooner or later she'll read enough to become an excellent reader. With this type of child you really do have to take the long view.

I think the other thing you do with this kind of child is rely heavily on comics and magazines. Provide them with lots of reading material they can read on the run, so to speak. They can read comics while they're grabbing a snack. They can look through magazines while flipping channels on the TV. Keep lots of quick reading material in places where they sit down, no matter how briefly. Reading material near food is, of course, crucial. With all the running around, they get hungry often. We had a bookcase in our kitchen for years, filled with *Richie Rich* comics and *Sports Illustrated* magazines. I'd put reading material in the car, also. They can page through *Mad* magazines on the way to their endless soccer games and hockey matches. We never really allowed reading at family dinners—it was our one time to be together and talk—but you can certainly encourage your children to bring books or comics when they're going to be stuck at long formal dinners because you don't have a sitter. Surely other dinner guests would rather see your son hunched over a *Batman* comic than building pyramids with all his eating utensils.

With this kind of active child, ingenuity is the key. And I think you'll find that when your child does become an enthusiastic reader, he'll be a lot easier to manage. Times when he has to sit still can now be filled with high-interest reading. And you might find that he reads with the same high, single-minded intensity that he uses for more physical activities.

So don't despair if you have the classic kid who can't sit still. You just need to be a bit more creative in the kinds of reading you find, and the way you slip it to him.

Kids who are very active aren't the only ones at high risk for never really getting into reading. Sometimes kids who are very visual, who are entranced with color and shape and movement, seem to turn on less easily to reading.

Very Visual Children Are Sometimes Slow to Come to Reading

My younger daughter is like this. She didn't just look at books when she was younger; she tried to reproduce the drawings. While my other kids would like books for the stories, she loved the pictures. I could take her anywhere as long as she had a pad of paper and some markers. She'd be happy for hours.

As it turned out, Molly also came very easily to reading,

but I think one of the chief reasons was that she was the third child, and I was just too tired, and casual, to care that she loved picture books way beyond the time when she could easily read other books. Of course, I see now that it was her love of art that kept her early picture books dear to her. She read, and studied them, again and again. Thank heavens I never did say, "Why don't you put those easy books away?" I think her enjoyment of them has a lot to do with her enjoyment of reading now.

It's pretty common for me, however, to have very artistic students who read very slowly and poorly. They dress with that wonderful flair, win all sorts of awards in their art classes, and are often conscientious and hardworking students. But they don't like to read, and I think the major reason is that reading is such a verbal activity. Sure, you look at the words on the page, but you process the information verbally.

So with a child like this you also need to make an extra effort. Like the athletic child, this child is gifted in other ways, but there's no reason he can't also love reading.

I think the thing to do, actually, is what I did just by happenstance. Molly was the youngest of three, so our house was loaded with all kinds of colorful children's books. When the older kids cleaned out their rooms, they dumped all the books they didn't want in her room. She was buried in picture books for years.

The other thing I noticed about Molly was that it was very important for her to own books. It seems to me that I took my older kids to the library more when they were little, but Molly wanted to own the books, to keep them, to look at them again and again. It may also have been important for her to have relatively fresh-looking books. Library books are read so often that they sometimes get a bit of a dingy cast. Neither I nor my other kids ever cared about this, but the appearance of books was always so important for Molly.

I notice now that she's older she loves teenage magazines.

She'll spend hours looking at hairstyles and clothes (and reading a little, I think).

If you have a child like this I think it's important to be aware of her love of color and shape and movement. If she's still young, you have a wealth of lovely picture books available to you, and I'd really splurge and make sure she had as large a collection as you can afford. Comic books are great too, because they use visual means to tell a story. If she's older make sure she has access to magazines of all sorts. Realize that she might not read as much as her less visual friends, but at least you can make sure that she loves reading and will read when she has a chance. With any luck she'll fall in love with some trashy romantic series and become an absolutely wonderful reader. Then, with the excellent verbal skills she'll develop, and the excellent visual skills she already has, she'll be able to do almost anything. Very visual boys seem most apt to go from comics to science fiction or fantasy. I think maybe these colorful worlds entice them, much like early, colorful pictures in their picture books.

So if your son or daughter doesn't naturally come easily to reading, if your child is very active or very visual, don't worry. A little sensitivity and ingenuity on your part should ensure that your child still acquires a love of books.

But what if your son used to spend hours and hours reading comics and Choose Your Own Adventure books but now does nothing but tinker with his computer? What if your daughter read every Sweet Valley book you could beg, borrow, or steal but now spends every free minute on the phone with her friends? There is another aspect to reading you need to be aware of.

Kids Go Through Stages, Reading Lots at Some Time and Little at Others

I think almost everyone goes through stages with reading. I know sometimes I read much more than I read at other times, for no particular reason other than that something else is taking all my attention. But I don't think I do this with the variability of a kid. Maybe I don't get as intensely immersed in things anymore, so I usually have some energy left for reading. But kids often experience situations with such energy-draining intensity that they can do nothing but try to cope with that situation.

Many of my students tell me that they stopped reading for pleasure when they got to high school. Of course, their time was usually more scheduled in high school; in addition to classes, many students work at jobs or play an after-school sport. But I think it's more than that. I think high school is a tremendous emotional adjustment for kids, and their batteries, so to speak, go on low when they finally have an unscheduled moment. I think it's why they are so likely to flop in front of the television, or go out and rent a movie.

Sometimes this starts in junior high. My junior high daughter got so engrossed with social situations that the hours she used to spend reading were spent on the phone. All of the social nuances of the day were extensively discussed with her friends. Even though this gets very frustrating for parents at times, I think this total immersion in social relationships is probably valuable. She needed to move away from me at some point and find confidants elsewhere. She needed to talk out all the trauma involved in being thirteen.

My point is that sometimes stages of life or events in life will be so overwhelming that your child will think of nothing else. How do you keep your child reading then?

Again, of course, you firmly remind yourself that you're

interested in the long view. You want this sixteen-year-old son to love reading long after his obsession with cars has faded. You want your fifteen-year-old daughter to love reading even after she no longer cares about the latest rock group. So don't be too intrusive and push reading on them at this point. If they've loved it before, they'll come back to it.

There are some little things you can do, however. Find magazines and nonfiction books about their current passion. My thirteen-year-old daughter would pick up anything that had to do with teenage relationships and common teenage problems. My older daughter can still be counted on to immediately devour any book on soccer. My son loves history. Historical fiction, or even straight history books, are a sure bet.

Certainly if your son is car crazy, you need to have lots of car magazines around the house. A basketball fanatic needs books and magazines about basketball. Your goal is to keep the habit and love of reading alive until your son or daughter has the time and energy for more sustained, varied reading.

The other thing I've noticed about kids at a time like this is that they usually don't have the emotion, energy, or time to go out and look for reading material. You have to provide much of it. So buy the sure winners—books and magazines you know they'll like—and take more chancy books out of the library. Then if they don't read them, they won't feel guilty, and you won't feel mad.

Remember, take it easy. Kids go through stages when they read less, some kids find reading a very foreign way to cope with understanding life, and some kids just have a hard time getting started with reading. But you're not going to panic. You're going to ensure your child enjoys reading. Basically, you're going to try to have your child form a habit of reading. You want your child to have a reading life-style.

Your Ultimate Goal Is that Your Child Form a Reading Life-style

I think dieting made the idea of life-style popular. It's pretty commonly accepted now that, to attain and maintain a healthy weight, it's not a terrific idea to eat only grapefruit and seaweed for three consecutive months. We know that maintaining a good weight is more complicated. You need to eat a healthy diet. You need to exercise. Most of all, you need to eat only for the right reason—you're hungry—rather than all of the other possible reasons—you're bored, you're depressed, you're nervous, or whatever.

And we know now that it isn't the numbers on the scale at any one time that are important: it's your whole life-style in regard to eating. You need to form habits of eating well, of moving around more, of turning to solace other than food during rough times.

I see reading the same way. It's not the current numbers on the California Achievement Test, or the Scholastic Aptitude Test, or your daughter's last British literature test that are important; your daughter's attitude and habits of reading are important.

So you're going to encourage daily reading by having irresistible reading material wherever your kids spend a lot of time—in the kitchen, in their bedrooms, in the den. Try not to complain when magazines and comics are three feet deep in their bedroom. Try not to panic when you get notices from the library saying books are five months overdue and the police are coming. This is all typical behavior of kids who love reading. They are signs that you're winning! Your kids are adapting to the reading life-style. It's a good sign when the bookshelves in their rooms start to overflow with paperbacks. Be glad when they appear tired and disheveled at breakfast because they couldn't put their latest horror novel down and read until three *a.m*—and then had nightmares. They're growing, they're learning, they're reading!

The rest of the book will deal with more specific problems, but just keep your main goal in view all the time. You want your children to love reading. You want them to adopt a reading life-style. Every other goal in regard to reading is secondary.

And I'm convinced that every child who can read at all— no matter how slowly or poorly—can achieve this goal.

To help make this happen, however, it's not only important for you to have your goals straight and to understand the importance of the long-term picture, it's also important for you to understand the stages children go through in acquiring avid-reading behavior. The next chapter will describe these stages.

5

READING STAGES

I KEEP TELLING YOU NOT TO BE WORRIED ABOUT READING tests and reading levels. That's because they are often deceptive. I've seen students who tested close to their grade level on reading tests but couldn't do the required reading for a high school English course. That's because they could read the short sections on a test but couldn't maintain the concentration to see a book through. They couldn't follow a long plot; they got characters mixed up. So their testing was very deceptive, and everyone was continually blaming them for being lazy and refusing to read.

And, of course, some very good readers simply don't test well—although I don't see this happening too much. Usually the kids tagged as very good readers who don't test well are conscientious students who don't read very much. They complete their assignments, but they're not actually very fluent readers.

But the real reason for being aware of reading stages is that knowledge of the stages gives you a sense of where your child is on the road to acquiring avid-reading behavior. Of course, not all kids go through these stages the same way. Some kids skip stages, others linger a long while in one and then race madly through others. And these stages aren't scientific: they're just my observations, gathered over twenty years of teaching, of the different kinds of reading habits different levels of readers seem to have. If you're lucky enough to have a child who just picked up reading naturally, from the first day of school, you probably don't have to worry about these stages. Kids like this seem to read everything at once. But in case your child is one of the thousands and thousands who read very little, who have been turned off to reading in school, these are the stages you should watch for.

Stage One: Leafing through Books and Magazines

We had some very low-level readers at the high school I taught at in Virginia, some as low as a second-grade level, one actually on a preprimer level. When I sat these students down with a supply of magazines and comic books, the behavior of the low-reading students was all the same: they leafed quickly through each magazine and comic. Some kids did this for weeks; others settled down to try to read a little after a few days.

This behavior baffled me at first, until I remembered how my own children used to leaf through their picture books. For years, really, before they started reading, they looked through books, "reading" them by following the pictures. I think preschoolers do this as a way of imitating parents— they pretend they're really reading—but this leafing through also makes them feel friendly toward books, makes them feel they're part of the literary world, so to speak. In Virginia, I figured out that this early leafing through magazines and comics I saw in poor readers served almost the same purpose. It was almost as if these students who had failed so unhappily in reading needed this time just to feel friendly with books again. They were also, of course, very uninterested in reading. Reading was not a means by which they had ever gained any valuable or interesting information. So I waited, and let them page through one magazine or comic after another. They looked briefly at the pictures and sometimes read a word or two. But they were careful, at first, not to let themselves get too involved.

I think it's important for parents to be aware of this stage. My main recommendation for parents of very low reading students is to start with magazines or comics, depending on the child's age. I'd go with comics if your child is much under fourteen (even books like the *Garfield* ones are great), and magazines, if he's getting up to fourteen or fifteen. *Mad* magazine is actually a good bridge between the two. If your son isn't really ready for magazines yet but is insulted by comics, get him *Mad* and *Cracked*, and *Crazy*, and all of the similar magazines. But you need to know that first your son or daughter will just page through what might be a very expensive purchase—some of the rock magazines, like *Billboard*, are not cheap—and then throw it back on the coffee table. You figure you spent five bucks on this magazine, and he glanced at it for five minutes. That's a dollar a minute for glancing time. Can you afford to have your son love reading?

Don't be discouraged! Keep buying magazines and comics he likes. Ask him what magazines he'd like subscriptions to. If he shrugs his shoulders and says he doesn't know, check out magazines and comics yourself that you think he'll find interesting. Believe me, there are magazines on every subject imaginable. Try to find one of those huge newsstands that have every magazine and comic you've ever heard of. Buy, buy, buy! Bring home lots and watch to see which ones he picks up. Get subscriptions to those. Keep telling yourself that a reading tutor charges at least thirty dollars an hour, and these magazines and comics will be *much* more effective in increasing reading skills.

It's tempting, at this point, just to take your son to the

newsstand and ask him to pick out some reading material. This doesn't work too well at the beginning because, I think, poor readers are reluctant to commit themselves to reading anything. If he buys a magazine, he's afraid he'll have to read it. Of course, if he does pick out a comic or two for you to buy, that's great. Remain cool but say casually, sure, you guess you can afford those. But be encouraged because it's a very good sign.

The other thing you'll start to notice is that he'll start collecting magazines and comics he likes and looking through them again and again. You'll see that that five-dollar magazine really does get more mileage. Some comics will even start to take on a rather worn appearance. A wonderful sign!

And, after a few days or weeks or months, you'll start to notice that he is really reading parts of these magazines, and probably all of the comics. Just be patient. It will happen.

The worst reader I ever had was a kid I'll call Jack. His mother called me the night before he was to enter my ninth-grade English class. He was sixteen and coming from a school that specialized in learning-disabled kids.

"Jack has a reading problem," she told me. "He reads very little. Just treat him like he's blind. If you send home the books he's supposed to read, I'll read them to him."

"What kinds of things does he read?" I ask her.

"Signs," she said.

I was blank for a minute, and then I had it. "You mean like STOP and GO?" I asked.

"That's right," she said sadly.

This happened way back when I had first started teaching in Virginia. Luckily, Jack was coming to the school I told you about in chapter 1, the school that gave me money for magazines and comics and anything else the kids would read. I decided that I wouldn't treat Jack as if he were blind. He wasn't! I'd find out if I could get him reading.

When he came, I tested his reading level just to see if his mother's assessment was accurate. It was right on target. He tested on a preprimer level. Mothers always know!

And then I really just turned him loose in my room. The rule was that when he had English with me he had to be sitting down looking at some reading material. I figured he was sixteen years old, most of his schooling spent in a place specializing in learning disabilities, and reading on a preprimer level—what did I have to lose?

After a while he started spending most of his time looking at the *Doonesbury* books I had brought in. These are not particularly easy reading, but they were the books that interested him the most. He'd study them and study them. Sometimes he'd ask me a word, sometimes he'd ask a friend. Pretty soon he was spending much of his free time up in my room looking at *Doonesbury* books. The part about Zonker talking to his plants really tickled him.

But school, of course, was very hard for Jack, and three years later, when he was nineteen, he decided to drop out. I tested him again right before he left. I got a fourth-grade, fifth-month level in reading comprehension.

Now I'm not saying he was ready for Harvard, but he was no longer completely illiterate. I encouraged him to keep on reading, *Doonesbury* or anything else, and told him that if he did, his reading skills would continue to improve. I haven't seen him since, but I'd love to know how he's doing. And he really showed me that allowing kids to just page through reading material—even material that seems too hard for them—can be the breakthrough that gets them reading.

Once your son is really reading the magazines or comics you're supplying, he's moved on to the second stage.

Stage Two: Reading Comics, Magazines, and Newspapers

Once your child is firmly into this stage, you can relax. You are assured, now, that he will eventually reach a certain level of competency in reading. A kid who loves comics, and then magazines, and then newspapers will probably be a reader all his life. Magazines and newspapers are bread-and-butter reading. Even during the times your child is overwhelmed by other parts of his life—like college courses, or a first love—he will usually continue to do at least this type of reading.

Comics and magazines have many advantages. They have short articles and stories that a poor reader can read in one sitting. They have pictures to help him guess the meaning of words he doesn't know. Most of all, they are essentially serial literature. If your daughter likes one *Archie* comic, you know that she'll love the next two hundred that you buy for her. After a while even a poor reader can read comics effortlessly. The characters are the same. The story line is essentially the same. The type of language and tone are the same. Your daughter can enter happily into a world she enjoys—Archie's high school experience—fully confident that every story will turn out the way she wants it to. Comics pass the test of being interesting, engrossing literature for a beginning reader, and the speed with which she can tear through comics will increase her self-confidence and help her see herself as a literate person.

And comics are reading that kids really enjoy being experts in. They collect comics. They trade them. They take great pride in reading all of one series that's available. Harvey House stopped publishing *Richie Rich* comics for a while, and when, after three or four years, they started appearing on the newsstands again, Julie was eager to try one.

"It's a reprint," she told me, and then laughed. "But I may be the only person that would know that!"

Magazines don't lend themselves to collecting with such a passion, but kids certainly do save the magazines they love. And some of them they read over and over. And magazines are a good lead-in to newspapers. After your son has been reading *Sports Illustrated* for a while, start leaving the sports section of the newspaper on the kitchen table. Be sure you get all the local papers—kids like most of all to read about the local sports teams, and all the other local happenings. *The New York Times* may have better news coverage, but their sports coverage of Concord–Carlisle High School can't compete with *The Concord Journal*, or *The Middlesex News*, or even *The Boston Globe*. So get local papers and leave them around.

My son wasn't very interested in sports in high school. No, Tim fell in love with my husband's *Wall Street Journal*. This was fine when he was at home, but it got expensive when he went away to college and ordered a subscription for himself. ("I considered just calling and doing a change-of-address on Dad's subscription," he told me, "but then I thought . . . ") But again, we're glad he's reading!

So keep encouraging comics, magazines, and newspapers. Newspapers and magazines are reading your child will do his whole life. But you do want your child to move on to books as well. Books demand more sustained attention than periodicals. Book reading develops skills that periodical reading doesn't. And, of course, there is a special enjoyment in curling up with a good mystery novel, or reliving the history of Israel in *Exodus*. Books deal with subjects in more depth. You want your child to be able to understand the thorough and complex treatment of a subject that only a book can give. So keep your children reading periodicals, but try to move them to books as well.

I should mention here that your son or daughter may have

been assigned books for school. I've had lots of kids over the years who have read the assigned books but not much else. If this has been happening, don't relax. That's not good enough, for a number of reasons. First, it's very possible your son hasn't enjoyed the books he's been assigned, so he's been learning to dislike reading, rather than to love it. Secondly, if your son has disliked the book enough, there's a very good chance that he hasn't even read it. You would probably be amazed, and horrified, to know how many kids slide through school reading very little, if any, of the assigned reading. And third, the books your son has been assigned in school don't usually lead to more reading. They're usually not series books or category fiction books. Even if your son does read and enjoy an occasional schoolbook, it is doubtful that that book will lead him into avid reading. So what follows are some suggestions for books, or types of books, that you should offer to your son or daughter. Some of these books I've given to literally hundreds of kids. There's a very good chance you'll find something that works for your child.

(In the Appendix I have given a more extensive list of suggested books for readers at varying levels of fluency. For now I'm discussing the kinds of works that work best for starting kids off as book readers.)

Stage Three: That First Book

Most of the books I'll be mentioning here are either series books, or category fiction, or both. This is so that if your child likes the book, it's easy to find the next book for him. You just continue the series!

Young children are easy. If your child is very young (under nine or ten) and really just moving out of picture books, you can probably move him into short chapter books, or even easier, into the Choose Your Own Adventure books. There are lots of series books for young children, everything from the Berenstain Bears books (which my younger daughter loved and read for years) to series about horseback riding, about sports, about almost everything. There was another series about a little witch named Dorrie (by Patricia Coombs) that both my daughters loved. If your child is still young and is reading fairly well, you shouldn't have very much trouble hooking him up with early books.

It gets harder when kids are older. They have a mind-set against reading. They've probably experienced a good deal of failure around reading in school. You'll find that it wasn't too hard getting them to read magazines and comics, but books are different. Books are more like school. Books seem like a waste of time to them.

So you need to choose this first book you give them very carefully. You want them to actually read it, and to read it with pleasure. The tricky thing is that books they could read with pleasure they will often look suspiciously at and declare are "too easy." They say this because their confidence in reading is so low that they pick up on any imagined slight. So I've tried to recommend books that are easy to follow but don't look like children's books.

A general rule when choosing books is that a first-person narrative is easier to follow than a third-person one, especially a third-person narrative that jumps around. Something else to look for: humor. Boys, especially, who dislike reading are often caught by a book that is funny. Other than that, it's a gamble, but I've tried to make it easier by mentioning some books that have worked for me in getting my students to enjoy reading.

Certain kinds of periodical reading lend themselves to certain kinds of book reading. For example, readers of superhero comics seem to move into fantasy and science fiction books. If your son has been happily reading comics, I'd try him with a short fantasy novel like *Another Fine Myth* by Robert Asprin. This is a short, funny opening book to a fantasy series, so if he likes it you can get him the six or seven other ones in the series. Hand the book to him, say you heard it was good, and then let it go. Sooner or later he'll be assigned a book report in school, or he'll run out of comics and be looking for something else to read, or he'll notice it on his bedside table and pick it up out of curiosity. If you're planning a long trip, give it to him then. Long car rides or plane rides or train rides get pretty boring. Maybe he'll open it for lack of anything else to do.

If you've gotten your daughter reading with *Archie* comics, then you want to try some novels about high school kids. Teenage romances are pretty much *Archie* comics in novel form. There are tons of these in any bookstore.

Magazines, of course, lead into nonfiction books. This is probably the easiest route to follow with boys over the age of about twelve or thirteen. Find books similar to whatever magazines they've been reading. If your son is interested in rock music, the infallible book is *No One Here Gets Out Alive*, by Jerry Hopkins and Daniel Sugerman. It's a biography of Jim Morrison, and for some reason teenagers who love rock music can't seem to put it down. There are a number of other rock-musician biographies out now, too. If your son likes Pink Floyd, for example, be sure to buy the book about that group.

Sports biographies are also sure winners for kids interested in a particular sport. Books like this almost have the allure of magazines, and it usually isn't a problem to get your son to pick one up. Just be sure it's about a player he likes.

If your son hasn't yet read enough magazines or comics to have adequate reading skills in place but needs to read a book for school, give him *The Outsiders* by S. E. Hinton. Along with *No One Here Gets Out Alive*, it's almost an infallible book for teenage boys. Plus it's short and easy to read. Or even if he doesn't need a book, give it to him. In fact, you might read it yourself. It's one of my own favorite teenage novels. Almost as good is S. E. Hinton's next book, *That Was Then, This Is Now*.

For girls the choice is broader. If your daughter is still under the age of thirteen or fourteen, definitely get a book from a series like the Babysitters, or the Nancy Drew series. The Sweet Valley series now has a sort of subseries for girls as young as seven or eight. These kinds of series are pure gold for developing readers.

If your daughter is older you might try some of the teen-age romances. One of my daughters really enjoyed them; the other wouldn't be caught dead with one. Girls like the S. E. Hinton books also, so you might give *The Outsiders* a shot. If your daughter is approaching fourteen or fifteen you could give her *Flowers in the Attic* by V. C. Andrews. This book has to be high on the list of infallible books for girls—and I've even seen boys hunched breathlessly over it. It's got everything—child abuse, incest, murder—but it's almost a surefire book it you're trying to get a teenage girl reading. And I figure they see this stuff on television all the time anyway. They might as well pick up a love of reading instead of a love of television watching. Other good authors for the important first book: Danielle Steel (one of her shorter ones, like *The Promise*). Robert Parker's Spenser mysteries—start with *Early Autumn* but tell your son or daughter to skip the first page, which is very boring and hard to read, and to start at the first full paragraph on the second page. Or you might try Piers Anthony. The first book of Anthony's wonderful Xanth series is the one to give your teenager. It's called *A Spell for Chameleon* and is wonderful except that the first couple of pages are difficult and boring. Tell your teen to skip them. (My daughter used to tell her friends to skip the whole first chapter. I wouldn't go that far. By the third or fourth page it's pretty good, and you need the information in the first chapter to easily follow the rest of the story.) The Xanth books are perfect for a teenager who has done a fair amount of comic or magazine reading. They demand a little more reading skill than the Robert Asprin Myth series. But I think they're also better—and there are about twelve or thirteen books in this series now. Some kids absolutely fall in love with the Xanth books. I had a sophomore boy once who, before I got him, had done mostly just magazine reading. He dallied along with me for a while, usually just reading a short story or two a week from some anthology he brought from home. Then I thought to hand him *A Spell for Chameleon*. Wow! He *loved* it and finished it in about a week. I found him the next book, and the next one. When he got toward the end of the series he started buying his own copies of the books, because I was usually out of them. Then a nice grandfather of his gave him all the books in the series that he didn't have for Christmas. Well! He immediately started reading the whole series again! Since then, when I see him, he's usually reading something—and waiting for the new Xanth book to come out. A really good thing about the Xanth series is that there are so many books in it that by the time a kid has read them all his reading is usually strong enough that he can go on to other, more sophisticated series, like the Shannara books by Terry Brooks, or one of the other series I'll list in the back.

Before leaving the "first book" section, I want to mention some books that *don't* work well. These are all wonderful books, but kids just moving into books rarely like them. These books seem to demand more sophisticated literary tastes. I'm mentioning them because they are titles that are often given to kids by well-meaning parents and teachers. You can try them after your child's love of reading is firmly entrenched. But not now!

The list: *Catcher in the Rye*, by J. D. Salinger, *All Quiet on the Western Front*, by Erich Maria Remarque, *Tom Sawyer* by Mark Twain, *A Separate Peace*, by John Knowles, *Catch-22*, by Joseph Heller, anything by Agatha Christie, Ayn Rand, Robert Cormier, Rex Stout, Virginia Hamilton—and anything written prior to the twentieth century, with the possible exception of *Huckleberry Finn* by Mark Twain.

I'm mentioning these books and writers specifically— there are *lots* more that don't work for unenthusiastic read- ers—because they are books you probably remember read- ing and loving. The natural inclination is to give them to your child. And later your son or daughter probably *will* love *Catcher in the Rye*, but not now. Let him have the experience of reading some books he can't put down before you hand him one of these old favorites. After all, you don't want to ruin *Catcher in the Rye* for him, do you? Or Agatha Christie? And I think that's what happens when a kid struggles through a book he really isn't ready for yet.

If you do need to give your just-into-books reader a "clas- sic" book for a school report, try *To Kill a Mockingbird* by Harper Lee. Almost every kid I've known loves that book. *The Hobbit* by J. R. R. Tolkien works well for some kids (boys more often than girls). *The Color Purple* by Alice Walker works well for my African-American kids—girls, es- pecially. *Black Boy*, by Richard Wright, works pretty well for the boys.

Again, I urge you to try the series books I've mentioned in the beginning of this section first, if you can. Because if your son or daughter enjoys a book that's part of a series, they have a place to go next.

Where they go next, of course, is on to the rest of the books in the series.

Stage Four: Very Narrow Reading

This can be a very frustrating stage. You've watched your child fall in love with a book. But now, rather than enthu- siastically reading all of the other books in the world, your daughter only wants to read the V. C. Andrews book that comes after *Flowers in the Attic*. Your son wants you to scour the bookstores for the next Robert Parker book. Nothing else will do.

You need to know that this is completely normal behavior. I've watched virtually all my kids who are just starting to read do this. *All* of them. It's got to be much easier for you as a parent, than for me as a teacher, because you can just go out and buy that next book. I can't afford to buy that next book for my hundred or so kids. I collect books like crazy at flea markets and yard sales, but I often end up really scrounging around for that next book. And that's all many kids will read. It's only after they've read every book in a series, or every book by a particular author, that they'll entertain the possibility of trying something new.

But I think that's okay. They're reading! They're enjoying the books! Go that extra mile and find that book they want. My son fell in love with Anne Rice's vampire novels a few summers ago, and I can remember driving from bookstore to bookstore looking for the one just out. Of course, it was just out in hardback, and cost about twenty dollars, but that was okay. What better thing could I be spending my money on?

Every so often I have a parent who will really floor me. The parent is willing to spend big bucks on clothes, sports, even a car sometimes, for his son—but he won't give him money to go buy books. My guess is that that parent just doesn't understand the critical importance to his son of getting the right book next. He thinks the kid might as well go to a library and pick up any book. He doesn't understand that it has to be this particular book in this particular series. A parent like this will often tell me that she doesn't need to give her daughter money for books—they have lots of books at home. Maybe, but I bet they don't have the new sequel to *Dawn* by V. C. Andrews—and there's a good chance that that is the only book her daughter will read now!

So resign yourself to the fact that this stage will cost you some time and money. Just keep telling yourself that it's the best investment you can make. Your child is reading.

After a while, of course, the inevitable happens, and the series, or author, runs out. Your daughter has read all the Danielle Steel books. Your son has read every sports biography you can find. There are no more unread Spenser novels left in the bookstores. Hopefully, by the time this happens, your child has discovered how much fun book reading is. He has a habit of reading now that doesn't just include periodicals. With his confidence in his ability to get through a book, and his habit of reading, you should be able to start branching him out.

Stage Five: Branching Out

You may think by now that your child is an independent reader that you can turn loose. Not so. Kids in this stage still need a lot of help finding books. I think the ability to continually supply oneself with books doesn't come in until the final stages of reading. Certainly, at this stage, it won't be there.

So you need to keep helping. Realize that, just because your son or daughter has gone through the initial series or author, they won't necessarily be willing to try many new books now. They'll really be looking for another new series or author that is just exactly like the series they've finished. That's what you're going to help them find.

And this isn't so strange. Most avid readers I know usually binge read—read all of an author or series before moving on to something else. The difference is that a real avid reader won't let the absence of a favorite author or series stop him. If he can't get the new Dick Francis, he'll find something else. Your child probably isn't at that stage yet.

So what do you try? At this point, I'd try to get my child more involved in finding books. If he loved the Xanth series, take him to the bookstore and show him where the fantasy section is. Suggest Terry Brooks as a new author, or let him browse for a while. Hopefully he'll spot something to his taste, and you, of course, will willingly buy it.

This is probably a good time to start using the library. Check out a lot of different books similar to the series your daughter has just enjoyed. Bring them home and tell her that she might enjoy one or two, but they're just library books, so if she doesn't want to read them, no big deal. You'll just take them back.

A word about library use: my own children, and my students in school, are really incredibly casual about returning books on time—or at all. For your own peace of mind, and to prevent ugly scenes in the home, you should just quietly take the responsibility yourself for getting books returned. Dig the books out from under their bed, behind the cushions on the couch, inside their schoolbags. Remember, you're glad they're reading! The occasional cost of a lost book is a small price to pay.

You may sometimes find yourself frustrated, while your son is at this stage, because *all* he wants to read is fantasy. All your daughter wants to read is bodice-ripper romances, or mysteries. But don't be, because my experience is that all avid readers have this love of a certain type of book that seems to remain part of their makeup. Even my wonderful British literature students, who can read Chaucer and Shakespeare with enjoyment, usually maintain their love of the genre that brought them to reading. I think that even adults are the same way. I loved Nancy Drew mysteries when I was nine, and I still always check out the new mystery section of the library every week. So don't be discouraged when you can't yet get your science fiction loving son to read *Trinity* by Leon Uris. He'll get there, sooner or later, if you support and encourage his reading of science fiction now.

Stage Six: Wider Reading

Your child is in this stage when he willingly picks up a book outside his usual category of reading. A number of things precipitate this. Let's say your daughter has been reading romances, and she's gone through all of the early teenager romances, like the Sweet Valley books, all of the V. C. Andrews books, all of Danielle Steel. Maybe she's taken a little detour and started into historical romances also, and read Kathleen Woodiwiss or Georgette Heyer. After all this reading, I can guarantee you that her reading speed has really picked up. Books don't last her as long as they used to. Much more frequently now, she's looking around for that next book.

And she's starting to grow out of some of her early authors. The great thing about Danielle Steel books, for slow readers, is that every twenty pages or so a major event happens: someone dies of cancer, a long-lost love shows up, people are divorced and remarried. So a slow reader hits a major event every hour or so when reading. A fast reader, however, hits a major event every fifteen minutes—and after a while the book becomes rather dizzying. It's when your daughter reaches this stage that she'll begin to enjoy books written at a more leisurely pace, and in a more thoughtful manner.

Certainly, by the time she is at this reading stage, she should be in high-level English classes, if the classes at her school are leveled. And she'll be assigned more sophisticated reading. When I assign a book like *Pride and Prejudice* by Jane Austen (an eighteenth-century classic) to my British literature class, my students who are avid readers, especially if they are girls, love it and want to go on and read more books by Austen. My students who don't do much independent reading find the pace of the book intolerably slow; they never want to hear the name Jane Austen again.

So if your daughter has been avidly reading books in her category for a while, the common school practice of assigning classic books will help to branch her out. She'll be ready for these slower-paced classic novels, and she'll find that she can enjoy books other than the ones in her special category.

Kids at this wider reading stage are also much more receptive to being given books by you. Bring home lots of books from the library or from a bookstore. Offer to share. Recommend books that you've enjoyed. This is a perfect time to hand *Catcher in the Rye* to your son, or *Jane Eyre* to your daughter.

One of my students who has been an avid reader since he was about three or four—and who has the most wonderful written language you can imagine—told me that his mother goes to a bookstore every couple of weeks and buys a bag full of paperbacks. When she comes home they make deals about who gets to read what first.

This may sound expensive to you, but consider: ten paperbacks cost between forty and sixty dollars. That's the price of a dinner out for two—if it's not an expensive restaurant. It's the cost of two or three trips to the local movie theater with your spouse. It's the price of one cotton blouse at a medium-priced department store.

So start bringing books home. Recommend to your kids the books you love. Read the books they recommend to you. If your son has been a Stephen King fanatic but enjoys the copy of *The Vampire Lestat* by Anne Rice that you hand him, you have all of the Anne Rice books to give him now. And they lead into historical fiction, particularly her book about pre–Civil War New Orleans, *The Feast of All Saints*. Historical fiction might lead him into espionage, and biography, and maybe even pre–twentieth century fiction and nonfiction. And it will quickly lead him to the next stage of reading.

Stage Seven: Independently Finding Books

This is a stage your child has probably been approaching for a long time. Your daughter has been picking up magazines in the supermarket. She's been looking for the sequel to *Heaven* by V. C. Andrews. Maybe she's moved into mystery series and wants another Mary Higgins Clark book. Perhaps she loved *Catcher in the Rye* in school and wants to read other books by J. D. Salinger. But you know that you're really home free when she takes off for the library or bookstore without a specific author or book in mind. She just needs *something* to read. She finds new authors. She tries new types of fiction. She starts bringing home nonfiction books on subjects she doesn't have a school report due on. She's just always reading, always looking for that next book.

This is when you *can* relax as a parent. Reading has become a necessary part of your child's life. Your son won't spend all his free time playing video games now. He'll still play them sometimes, but he'll always go back to reading. Your daughter may forget about books temporarily when she's over her head in a demanding premed course in college, but she'll go back to pleasure reading. I don't think a love of books ever leaves a person. Bookstores will always beckon. A plane ride without a book will always be unthinkable. Life will be richer.

And your child will become firmly entrenched in the last stage.

Lifelong Avid Reader Stage

When your child is continually seeking out new authors, when his bookcases are always crammed full, when he thinks nothing of dropping fifty dollars of your money (or even his) in a bookstore, when he can't eat breakfast without reading the paper, when he reads two, or three, or ten books at the same time—you have a lifelong avid reader.

And I think when this happens you have a fundamentally changed person. You have a child who is continually absorbed in other people's perspectives, in other people's view of the world. One of my students, who is well on her way to avid reading, described her experience of reading a book about a disturbed child, called *One, Two, Three*, by Eleanor Craig: "When I read this last part, I felt really happy. I wasn't expecting such a good ending after I had gone through everything with the characters and felt frustrated when the subjects had a relapse. I felt that I had in some way helped because I was there when everything happened. And I felt pleased when Nellie and Matt had improved so much."

I love the fact that she felt she was there when it all happened, and that she had in some way helped. I don't think you get that experience from a movie. Movies go by so fast. And other people watch movies with you. Reading a book puts you in a personal, one-to-one relationship with an author.

And when you get your child to this last stage, you'll have put him into a personal, one-to-one relationship with books.

The next chapter gives hints on how to set up your house to make it more reading-friendly.

6

CREATING A READING-FRIENDLY HOUSE

OKAY, YOU HAVE THE GENERAL PHILOSOPHY IN MIND of how to make reading enjoyable. You're going to find easy, engaging reading material, you're going to treat your child's reading choices with respect and interest, you're going to recognize what reading stage he's in, and you are, very adroitly, going to help him progress through the stages.

The best help to doing all this is having a reading-friendly house. To have a reading-friendly house, there are conditions you're going to have to accept.

Reading Isn't Neat

When my oldest daughter, Julie, was about one and a half, she could be counted on to do one thing every time she was in the living room: she pulled all the books she could reach out of the bookcase onto the floor. Every day! This was sort of a drag until I realized that she just wanted to be handling books all the time, as she saw me doing. Her books, my books, it didn't matter. She liked to have *books* to mess around with.

Things didn't get any neater when she got older. Picture books everywhere—on the floor, under her covers, in the hall. Then the comic book era began, and I actually found comics on the stairs a few times. Did she stop to read when she was coming down to breakfast? For years, comics were everywhere. My second two children came along, and the scattered reading material grew exponentially. On the floor in front of the television—*how* did they read with cartoons blasting?—in the car, all over their bedrooms, and of course, always in the kitchen. I had a bookcase in the kitchen, but the bookcase was always a mess to start with, and only a fraction of the comics or magazines actually seemed to land there.

In a reading-friendly house, reading material just accumulates. It seems to be everywhere! A couple of years later we moved to a smaller house. We had spent ten years in a big old house with five bedrooms and a walk-up third floor. Well! The books! There was no way all these books would fit into our new house. And we no longer had a picture book reader. Boxes and boxes of books were sold at garage sales, given to neighborhood kids, and donated to libraries and Goodwill. It was heartbreaking, wrenching—but we *still* had way too many books.

I used to think that all these books all over the place were just due to my inept management, but I've been in too many other houses of readers since then. It seems that when readers get their houses to a tolerable level of neatness, more reading material floods in. Magazines! Newspapers!

We live right down the street from the Concord Public Library now, and that's helped a lot. I try to get most of my reading out of the library (except for current magazines, newspapers, best-sellers I can't pass up, great finds at flea markets . . .), but libraries never helped me too much with my children. Much of the reading they loved (comics, magazines, Sweet Valley books, Xanth books, the Anne Rice books *in order*) either couldn't be found in the library—or were books my kids wanted to own.

I know this is an issue for some parents, and I sympathize. Being one of five children myself, and having a lovely, relaxed mother, I can tolerate a good deal of clutter, especially if it's for a good cause, like reading. But I know some people just can't. I actually had a student, from a very affluent family, tell me one time that they didn't get a newspaper because her mother said newspapers were too messy. Not surprisingly, this girl was not a very good reader.

Neatness is an odd quality. Almost every other quality we want our children to acquire—enthusiasm for work, ability to feel compassion and form relationships, love of life—children acquire naturally if they are truly loved, and truly helped to be independent. But neatness? Some kids, of very lucky parents, seem to be born neat, and some kids seem to acquire an early love of order. But most children leave their childhood strewn with Legos in the carpeting, doll clothes under the coffee table, magic markers on the dining room table—and books and comics everywhere.

What do you do if you are a very neat person? Is it possible to have a completely neat, clean, orderly house—and a child who loves reading?

I'm not sure it's possible to have an *entire* house that is neat, clean, and orderly. I think you have to tolerate at least a little disorder in certain areas. Certainly in your children's rooms, for example. Better books under the bed sometime, than books that are never taken out of the bookcase. Let me tell you about some of my experiences with casual, mess-tolerant parents, and see if I can convince you that absolute neatness is not always a virtue.

Through all my years of moving around, following a navy husband, I've been in a lot of houses. I've had a lot of friends, of the neat and the not-so-neat variety. My friends who tolerated a certain amount of clutter in their homes just seemed to have children who were more enthusiastic about everything, including reading.

I remember J. P., in Norfolk. He was the youngest of ten children and lived in a big, old house. As his older brothers

and sisters left home, he expanded his collection of *stuff*—
books, experiments, art supplies, building materials. He
took over some of their bedrooms, the back porch, the yard.
And he read everything. When I met him he was in fourth
grade and reading *The Man Who Never Was*, an adult book
describing a World War II intelligence operation.

And then there are the children, in the last neighborhood
we lived in, who have a mother who helps them fill their
house with plants that have caterpillars growing on them,
piles of dress-up clothes scrounged from the town dump—
"My mother says these are *perfectly* okay," the little girl explained to me—and books from garage sales, flea markets,
libraries. They read in the books all about the caterpillars,
the plants, and heaven knows what else. It's a house
friendly to children, and friendly to books.

And even if the teenagers I get from these casual, project-
filled homes aren't into reading yet, it's pretty easy to move
them in that direction. I had one boy who raised birds and
knew everything there was to know about the subject. To
learn all of this, he had read from cover to cover all of the
pamphlets and direction booklets his parents had found for
him. When I gave him a Robert Parker novel, he already
had the reading skill to read it—and he had parents who
were used to encouraging his projects. They were glad he
was reading and so went out and bought all of the Spenser
novels he wanted.

I think the top Parent Award for Allowing Messy Projects
goes to the mother of one of my colleagues. She allowed
her daughter to spread a tarp over the expensive wall-to-
wall carpeting in her bedroom, load it with topsoil—and
grow grass. Yes. And her daughter, an avid reader, later went
on to Harvard.

I have the other kind of stories, too. There was the boy
whom I was seeing after school because the class he was
assigned to with me wasn't working very well for him. So I
met him after school, and we read books together. Of

course, I had to get him all the books; his mother wasn't used to doing that sort of thing. Once I told him I had forgotten the book he wanted.

"You know how it is," I told him. "It was on my dining room table with a bunch of other stuff, and I just didn't notice it in the mess."

"No, I don't know," he told me. "There's never anything on our dining room table. Our whole house is always completely neat."

"Even your room?" I asked him.

"My mother says it's her house so even my room has to be completely neat."

This was a very unhappy kid, who had been thrown out of a couple of private schools, and was now almost failing out of the public high school. But he lived in a neat house!

I'm not saying you have to let your children plant grass on their wall-to-wall carpeting, but I do think that if you want your children to have a joyous, easy relationship with books—and with learning in general—you have to tolerate a certain amount of disorder. You have to let your kids have some control over their environment—and that will probably mean piles of magazines here, lots of sporting equipment over there.... Just keep saying to yourself, in eighteen years they'll go away to college.

Reading Is Expensive

I've already talked about this a bit: you need to buy those early magazines and comics. You need to buy the next book in whatever series your kids are reading. As they read more and more, it's good just to come home with lots of books that the two of you can read together.

But I haven't talked much about the philosophical implications of this. I teach in a pretty affluent town, and the teenagers I have are very attuned to the influence, the effects, and the importance of money. When they read a book, they might miss some of the more subtle issues of social class, or stereotyping, or power games—but they never miss the money issues. Reading *Ordinary People*, they notice that Conrad's mother buys him new clothes because she's concerned about how his appearance affects her reputation, and because buying him something is easier than talking to him or spending some time with him. A student brought in a clip from the movie *Less than Zero* in my Exploring Issues Through Literature class—and the class immediately commented on how the parents had given the kids cars, clothes, presents—but no time or love. When we read *Early Autumn* by Robert Parker, the kids point out that Paul's parents don't even care enough about him to see that he has any decent clothes. Spenser has to buy him decent clothes from his own money.

They see that money cuts a number of ways. Some parents, they think, spend money rather than time or love on kids. Other parents don't even value their kids enough to buy them the essentials. But no matter how they see money working, spending money carries weight with my students.

I have many students who go south, or to ski country, on every school vacation. The expensive cars in the parking lot tend to belong to students, not teachers. Their clothes are from the Gap; their haircuts are from little salons in Concord Center.

And their books are books I buy for them at flea markets.

I used to find this strange. I, who drive a six-year-old Chevy station wagon, with rust on the bottom and a glove compartment that won't stay closed, have to buy, out of my extravagant teaching salary, the books for kids who drive Volvos.

I'm not angry about this, particularly; I'm just saddened that so many well-educated, well-meaning parents don't understand the first thing about books and money. These are some of the things they don't understand:

To say to a kid, "Well, go to the library if you want a book," isn't good enough: as I've explained, libraries don't carry, or have enough of, the kind of reading that makes kids fall in love with books.

To be willing to spend money on books shows that you value books. To be willing to spend $2000 on a ski vacation, and not $6.95 on a paperback, sends a disturbing message to your children. And children pick up on this; believe me, children know that—to paraphrase the Bible—Where your treasure is, there is where your heart will be. They know that you spend money on what you value.

Spending money on books isn't a suspect form of spending. I've never heard a kid say, "Oh, her parents don't care about Julie. They buy her books all the time as a substitute for spending time with her." Kids know it takes time to pick out books and magazines, and that you're hoping to find something they'll enjoy reading. Kids know that you don't buy books or magazines as a sign of status, always a worry if you join expensive clubs or send your kids to expensive private schools. No kid thinks for a minute that you're buying that copy of *The National Enquirer* for him, at the supermarket checkout, to gain *status*. He knows perfectly well that you're only embarrassing yourself like that—hoping the clerk can slip it into a grocery bag before a neighbor happens along—because you really care about him finding enjoyable reading material. You don't subscribe to *Disco Rollerskating* as a status symbol.

Kids, like everyone else, always want to be loved for themselves. Being willing to spend money on their tastes in books and magazines is a powerful message that you value their tastes, that it's okay for them to like superhero comics or *Mad* magazine.

So you do need to spend money on books: so your kids will have access to the fairly junky reading they'll learn to love books with, so they'll see you value reading, and so they'll understand that you think their taste in reading material is just fine, thank you. Buy them books. Give them money for books. Order all the local newspapers they'll read. Subscribe to every junky magazine they show an interest in.

In doing this, of course, you'll be far from the mainstream. Most people simply don't understand the importance of spending money on books. You don't believe me? Just ask yourself this: when school budget cuts are announced, what would draw the biggest crowd of protesters? Cuts to the school library, or cuts to the athletics budget?

A word here about school librarians: most school librarians I know are on the front lines every day in the war against illiteracy. I've seen librarians make valiant efforts to find just the right book for the right kid. But the wealthy town I live in doesn't seem to value school librarians. None of the elementary schools or middle schools even *have* a librarian any more. They were all cut, replaced by library aides.

Kids notice these messages. This society is willing to spend money on activities it values. So make sure that, in your home, reading is one of the most valued activities. Spend money on it!

Besides money, the other extremely valuable commodity in our society is time. And this is something else people don't seem to understand about reading:

Reading Takes Time

For most people, I think, the ideal teenager spends his time as follows: he plays at least one varsity sport, he participates in two or three other extracurricular activities or clubs, he holds down a job, he takes demanding courses, and he gets consistently high grades. During vacations he either works longer hours or takes a family vacation to the ski slopes in Colorado or to his grandparents' house in Florida.

What he doesn't do is sit on his front porch reading *The Firm* by John Grisham.

We worry about our kids just sitting around with nothing to do but get into trouble. And reading, somehow, doesn't count as a legitimate activity. At least it's not an activity our society seems to regard as a valuable use of time.

Look at the schools. How many hours a week, in school, do your kids spend reading books of their own choice that they really enjoy?

Probably none, is the answer. If they read in class, it's probably as a group, and they're all reading the same, teacher-assigned material. It's marginally okay to spend class time reading recognized classics, but it's not okay to let kids spend class time reading any old thing they want. Reading, on its own, isn't a valued activity—even in school! I've always thought this was odd, because working on math problems is okay to do in class. It's okay to work on science experiments in class. It's even okay to write in class. But read? There's the uneasy feeling that reading is maybe a waste of time, at best a filler, not an end in itself.

And let me tell you, kids pick right up on this. "I couldn't read last night," they tell me. "I had too much homework."

"Reading *is* your homework," I remind them, but they look dubious. Reading? Reading couldn't be as important a use of their time as doing math problems or history questions.

And I think we sometimes convey this attitude as parents. We try to keep our kids busy, signing them up for all sorts of sports and activities. We want to keep them occupied. We want to keep them out of trouble.

But we end up keeping them from reading. Reading takes a lot of time, particularly when kids are just starting. They read so slowly, you see, that if they only have twenty minutes here and there to read, they quickly forget the first part of the story. And they forget how much they were enjoying it.

One of my new readers explained it like this during a class discussion: "When I'm reading the book I'd rate it an eight," he said, "but then after I've put it down I forget how good it was and it only seems like a five or a six. It makes me not want to pick it up again."

A couple of other kids immediately chimed in, "Yeah!" That's how it was with them, also. They don't have much time to read, so the little bit of time they give to reading isn't enough to hook them.

So a major aspect of a reading-friendly house is that it's a house where people see reading as a legitimate activity. It's okay for your daughter to spend her Saturday morning lying across her bed, reading old issues of *Seventeen* magazine. It's okay for your son to drop out of his hockey league and spend his time after school organizing and reading his *Batman* collection. Reading takes time. You need to ensure that your children have this extra time in their schedule.

Actually, I think this just-reading-is-a-waste-of-time attitude is behind all the furor over politically correct literature for our children. Maybe reading isn't a waste of time if children are reading about a sensitive Japanese woman umpire who adopts a biracial special-needs child. Then reading is useful: it can be used to indoctrinate children. But just reading light fiction for entertainment? Surely our children would be better off spending the time chasing a soccer ball.

But, of course, they wouldn't—for all the reasons I mention in chapter 1.

Katha Pollitt makes this point eloquently in an article published in the December 1991 *Harper's* magazine, where she points out that the debate over which books students should be required to read is so bitter because books are seen as tools of indoctrination, and everyone wants students indoctrinated with a certain viewpoint. And yet the real problem is that so few students have an independent reading life, and "if you don't have an independent reading life—and very few students do—you won't *like* reading the books on the list and will forget them the minute you finish them." She uses the wonderful analogy that "while we have been arguing so fiercely about which books make the best medicine, the patient has been slipping deeper and deeper into a coma."

Helping a child build an independent reading life isn't a waste of time. So how do you find the time for leisurely reading in your child's schedule?

Of course you want your children to do activities that they really enjoy. Look for those activities that your children seem to be tiring of. Let's say it's spring soccer. I don't think I'd say, "Don't sign up for spring soccer. I want you to have time to read." Kids are such ornery creatures. That statement would probably ensure that they never picked up any reading material that whole spring, whether or not they played soccer.

You have to be more subtle. Let's say your daughter is signed up for Little League softball. Maybe her older sister played. All the kids in your family have always played softball. But you're getting the idea that your daughter doesn't really love the sport; she's too relieved when it's raining on a game day. Maybe the game will be canceled! She's too hard to get up on Saturday morning for a nine o'clock game.

Say to her, "I just don't have time to drive you to so many activities. I'm sorry, honey, I really am. But I just can't!" Or maybe you tell her you can't afford to have her in all those activities (you're spending your money on books, remember?) or something else has come up that you need to do on weekends . . . whatever! But the point is, you're not going to tell her that you want her to quit because you don't think she's that interested anyway. Then she'll feel bad— her sister was wonderful at the game. She'll think she should hang in and try. So think up another reason, and take the guilt on yourself.

Perhaps, however, you'll have a child like my older daughter, who simply loved sports and played at least one every season. That's harder, but we worked out a couple of things. One, she couldn't fill up every block of her schedule at school. I always wanted her to have at least one study period a day. Then she wasn't always loaded down with homework when she finally arrived home from whatever sport she was playing. In addition, we let her choose her own courses but put no pressure on her at all to take honors sections, even when her teachers were suggesting she go up a level. Honors courses are incredibly time-consuming. When she chose not to take an honors-level course, we supported her decision. And we told her we didn't want her working, even at a very part-time job.

This really set her apart from her friends. Most teenagers work now. When I was in high school, back in the early sixties, I can't remember any of my friends working. Now a great many teenagers hold down some kind of job, often during the school year.

I'm certainly not opposed to teenagers working, but it's so exhausting and time-consuming. Watch the kids at McDonald's. They're rushing around almost the whole time they're at work. After four or five hours of this, no wonder they want to go home and fall asleep on the living room floor in front of the television.

And most kids I know don't really have to work to put food on the table. They work to buy their own cars, to get a CD player, to buy clothes, to have money for movies or a dinner at Pizza Hut. Many work because we, as parents, have come to think that it's somehow *wrong* to give kids their spending money. Or it's wrong not to make them earn a good part of their college expenses while they're still in high school.

I have a big problem with this attitude. Of course we don't need to—and probably we shouldn't—give a kid enough money to get everything he wants in the way of stereo equipment and cars and clothes. But is it such a big deal just to give him some spending money? To make sure that when his friends are all eating dinner at Burger King and then going on to the school dance that he has the money to do that too—without working twenty hours a week, for minimum wage, at some dry-cleaning store?

Obviously, if you don't have the money to buy your child this kind of freedom from minimum-wage jobs, you don't. Then he's going to have to flip hamburgers, or whatever. But if you *can* give him a bit of spending money, and save for his college education yourself, you buy him time to read, and work on his own projects, and dream, and do all the kinds of things kids don't seem to have time for anymore. He'll have to work his whole life. Does he really have to start at the age of fifteen?

And if your son or daughter is in a school with ability-grouped classes, always keep in mind how much time top-level courses take. Maybe your daughter absolutely *loves* biology and doesn't mind spending fifteen hours a week memorizing all the details assigned in that course. Let her sign up! But don't you pressure her to. If she'd rather take a lower-level course and have some time to read her Danielle Steel novels, fine. Ultimately, she'll probably end up better educated.

A friend of mine—a wonderful person who has written some forty books and is one of the best teachers I know—says that what made her so literate was going to a lousy high school. "I had lots of time to read," she points out.

So you're going to try to ensure your child has the time to fall in love with reading. You don't want him always rushing off to a hockey game, or a soccer match, or a minimum-wage job. You want him to have lots of time to sit around your casual, comfortable, book-filled home. And read.

But what if you're willing to live with books piled everywhere, if you're willing to spend money on reading material, you're willing to give your kid lots of free time—and all he wants to do is sit around and watch television all day? That's a whole other chapter.

7

TELEVISION AND READING

THIS IS THE CHAPTER I'VE HAD THE MOST TROUBLE WRIT-
ing. What does a parent do about television? As one of my
students said, "Well, my mom thinks it corrupts my mind
and I should read much more, but I still watch a lot of TV.
I had a lot of fights about TV."

Again, I think it's important to be clear about long-range
goals. Do you want a child who watches only a little television and reads—but only because you're standing over
him with a sledgehammer? Or is your ultimate goal to have
a kid who says what another one of my students said: "Did
TV have an impact on my reading? Well no. I read because
I like to read, and I think reading is much better—I'd rather
imagine my own characters and places than see them on
TV."

I think I can assume that the second student embodies
the goal everyone strives for. We want kids who aren't very
interested in television and are very interested in reading.
But how do we get there?

Throughout the years, whenever I've been unsure about
how to teach a book, or structure a writing assignment, or
run a class discussion, I've asked my students their opinion.
Their advice is invariably better than that of any school ad-
ministrator or educational expert. So this year I started ask-

ing them about television and reading. Was television restricted in their homes? Did their television watching influence the amount of reading they did? What advice would they give to parents? Their answers have been fascinating for me, and from their comments, I've tried to sort out the television dilemma. What follows is the television *vs.* reading equation as I've gleaned it from my classes.

Most interesting question: did the wonderful readers watch much television?

Many of the Best Readers Report Not Being Very Interested in Television

"I never watched TV when I was younger. We had a TV but I never found an interest in watching it," one of my excellent British literature students reported. She said television was never restricted but "I love reading and would rather spend my time reading than watching soap operas on TV!!" The student also noted that her mother is a professor and "always encouraged me to read."

Another excellent student reports that "neither I nor my brothers were ever encouraged to read or restricted from watching television. However, I always liked to read and would spend hours in my room, reading everything that Paula Danziger, Judy Blume and Lois Duncan ever published—I seldom watched TV."

One student noted that television was not restricted at her house because her "parents decided that we would get bored of TV after a while." That usually happened "after a week or two" of summer vacation. Then she started doing a lot of reading.

One of my avid-reading sophomores reported that "TV has never been really restricted in my home ... [but] I never had much interest. TV is not something I really watch. My mother *makes* me watch *The Wonder Years* because she thinks it's educational."

But although a number of these wonderful readers re-ported choosing not to watch much television, in many cases the relationship between television watching and reading wasn't very clear.

There Is No Clear Relationship Between the Amount of Reading and the Amount of Television Watching Children Do

This is something I initially found hard to credit, but enough kids have described to me how they didn't read and didn't watch television—or did read and did watch televi-sion—that I'm forced to believe them. Some comments:

"I never really had the opportunity to watch what I wanted. I was always out with friends, or having a hockey game or soccer game.... One might think that I might have resorted to reading, but on the contrary, I never did, and ... I still don't like it."

"TV was not restricted at my house at all.... My best friend had to write down the exact hours that the TV was on and was restricted to two or three hours a week, and she didn't read any more than I did."

"I have a little sister and she reads a book a day *and* watches a lot of TV."

"There was never a limit on my television, but I never (and still don't) watched that much. My brother, on the other hand, watches TV like a champ, even though he has a TV limit (a half hour a night). My brother also enjoys reading and reads a great deal more than I ever did."

One of my avid-reading students reports that "even though I wasn't allowed to watch TV I didn't get into read-ing until seventh or eighth grade because I always had other things to do with other kids in the neighborhood, like baseball, football, soccer." He told me that his parents relaxed the TV watching rules right before he started high school, and ironically, that was when he started doing so much reading.

Another student: "As a child I watched quite a lot of TV. A minimum of three hours per day. Except Saturday when I watched at least five to six hours." But he went on to say, "This TV watching did not affect my reading in that if I was not watching TV I would *not* be reading. But that's 'cause I couldn't really read anyway."

So it's hard to figure. Restricting TV didn't necessarily lead to an increase in reading; allowing unlimited TV didn't slow some readers down at all. Having established that, I think it's important to mention that a number of my students thought they would have read more if they hadn't watched so much television.

A Lack of Television Will Sometimes Encourage Reading

I've heard stories from kids about reading their first book while they were away at camp. "I read the whole Narnia series," one boy confided to me. "There wasn't anything else to do." The son of a neighbor of ours didn't start reading until the family went camping for a year in Europe. He had been a television addict, but after a year without any television at all, he never went back to watching it. He became a reader instead.

One of my students described how she didn't do much reading until the summer she worked as a lifeguard. "There were many days when I'd be sitting around on break doing nothing, so I'd read. I read several books this summer because I had the time and nothing else to do. Having no TV around helped a little too, I think."

One of my students is sure that he would have read more without television: "I have never had restrictions on my TV. I have watched TV a lot since I was a baby. I never read a complete book before this English class. Television definitely has had a direct affect on my reading."

Another student says simply, "To be honest, I think I would have read more when I was younger if we had not had a TV. . . . I think people are better off without TV."

Another student: "My two brothers and I were not allowed to watch TV. . . . We all read until our eyes turned blurry; we'd go to the library every two weeks with a pile of books to return."

And finally: "In my house, the TV is always on, I'm not sure why. And I bet my brother and I would read more if it weren't constantly on."

What I gather from all this is that, although many kids read a lot *and* watch TV, a number of other kids feel that they really would read more if there wasn't any television in their house. So what do you do? Do you restrict television? This was probably the one aspect of reading and television that my classes were most in agreement about. Their opinion?

Restricting Television Watching Often Doesn't Work

"When we were little," one girl wrote, "my mom was always telling us not to watch TV and she made rules like we could watch half an hour of TV for every hour of reading we did. But it definitely did NOT work."

While some kids seemed to accept restrictions of TV watching, and the restrictions seemed to work ("My mother used to let us watch television *just* an hour, and both my sister and I used to love and still love reading"), many others tell me they simply circumvented the no-television rule.

They watched television at a friend's house, or at their own house when their parents were away. "My parents are seriously restricting our TV watching, but . . . my sister seems to watch it every day, despite all the NO TV signs my parents tape all over the TV."

And restricting television can cause problems: "I used to be obsessed with television when they restricted 'when' I could watch. Then I got a TV in my room and now I don't watch at all. It's too boring."

Another girl commented, "I remember [my mother] used to nag me to turn off the television and read. She used to make me read for an hour every day. I hated it. Reading is boring."

So restrictions can backfire. In some cases kids didn't seem to mind and ended up great readers, but in other cases the attempt to restrict television made the kids angry, seemed to turn them off to reading, and just encouraged them to ignore the rules.

What to Do?

Although some kids did report watching a good deal of television *and* reading, they were more the exception than the rule. It seemed that, by high school anyway, most avid readers simply weren't spending a lot of time sitting in front of a television. But it was also clear that restricting television often wasn't a good answer. That caused resentments, and sometimes—if the kids were told to read instead of watching television—caused a dislike of reading. One student explained to me that her mother used to turn off the television and send her to her room to read. "Reading was always work for me," she said. "I still feel like reading is work."

I've noticed another aspect to restricting television. A number of my students who report having had television restricted are good readers but are also quiet and passive in class. I'm not sure why this is. Perhaps their parents exerted a good deal of control in many areas of these kids' lives. Whatever happened, I find many of these students lacking in self-confidence. I think this is a pretty high price to pay to get your child away from the television—especially since many of my avid television watchers reported not reading much anyway.

So what can you do? This is what I would suggest:

Keep the Television off as Much as Possible with Preschoolers

Here's my thinking. It's pretty easy to simply maneuver small kids around. "*Now* it's time to go to the park! Shall we see if James wants to come too?" Have lots of toys around. Make many trips to the library. Import playmates, if you need to. With preschoolers, I think you can ensure they spend relatively little time in front of that screen without your having to make strict rules. If they watch sometimes, fine. But always try to arrange their lives so they're doing something else. If you're clever and adroit about this, I think you can manage it without the kids ever realizing that a major goal of yours is to keep them from vegging out in front of the tube.

I know that it's during the preschool years that it's most tempting to park kids in front of the television, since it's when kids are little that they have to be watched every minute. Television seems to be a godsend when you're trying to cook dinner, or fold laundry, or just have a minute to yourself. And letting them watch a little television is probably good—it keeps it from being something forbidden and glamorous. But I really think it's best, when children are little, if you can get them used to doing other things. It's good if you can get them to amuse themselves. Keep lots of paper and (washable) markers around, visit a thrift store for dress-up clothes, let the kids help you when you're cooking or doing laundry.

The goal is to help them develop the self-confidence that comes from *doing* things—building a block tower, flushing Legos down the toilet. Don't make a big deal of the television. It's there. Sometimes they feel like watching it, but you're glad that they're usually just too busy to sit and stare. Plus, you need help now with the chocolate-chip cookies you're making! *Someone* has to pour in those chocolate chips.

And a word of caution here. If your children attend a nursery school or day-care center, I'd drop in at inopportune times—for a lot of reasons, but noticing television use is certainly one of them. One of my children attended a day-care center once where they put all of the toys on high shelves in the late afternoon and sat all the kids on the floor in front of cartoons—for two hours! Needless to say, they had my business for *one* day.

Later on, in this book, I explain how, and why, you should teach your preschooler to read. One of my students actually mentioned that his babysitter taught him to read before he went to first grade, and he thought that was a major reason that he has always preferred reading to television. So you might do this too.

And, of course, you're going to be reading to your preschooler—wherever and whenever you get the chance. I really think most preschoolers would rather be snuggled up with mommy or daddy looking at a book than staring, all by themselves, at a television screen.

It's Harder to Discourage Television When Kids Get Older

By the time kids are seven or eight, they know what's on when, and they know what they want to watch. Plus friends talk about programs in school and invite them to their houses after school. A major theme of my students who had parents who restricted television was that they would just go to a friend's house and watch. And they seemed to do that completely without conscience. They can't watch at home? No problem. Saunter across the street!

This makes me nervous for a couple of reasons. I've already mentioned that I'm afraid this kind of overt parental control can cause problems with self-confidence. But the teacher in me has another worry. I simply don't like rules that kids routinely break. The way I keep discipline, and a good spirit of friendliness and camaraderie in my classroom, is by having very few rules, but enforcing absolutely the rules I have. Kids can come a minute or two late; they can leave to get a drink if they feel they need to; they can occasionally turn in a paper late. But they can't harass each other. They have to treat their classmates respectfully. They have to maintain a "civility of discourse." And I find that this method—few rules that you really enforce—works very well for me. So I'm nervous about a lot of restrictive television rules that the kids seem to feel very free to break.

But if you don't restrict television, how do you ensure that your son doesn't grow up with a remote control welded to his hand? Some suggestions:

If Your Child Is Watching a Lot of Television But Also Reading a Lot, Relax

My guess is that if your child is watching much television *and* reading, you have a pre–high school age child. I think some children go through a stage of watching a lot of television. As long as they are also willing, happy readers, you might do more harm than good by making draconian television rules. This doesn't mean that every so often you don't get *a little upset* and exclaim, "Would you turn that *#*#

thing off and go outside and play! Or go read a good book!
You look brain dead!" Of course you'll say that occasionally.
Everyone does. It's probably good. It lets your kids know
that, even though you're generally tolerant and easygoing
and trusting of them, basically you feel that people who sit
in front of television all day inhabit the vegetable kingdom.

I find that, by high school age, few avid readers have
much time for television. My daughter Molly, who's thirteen, explained to me that the books she can read now are
so much more absorbing than the children's books she used
to read that television is simply slipping into second place
as an entertainment source. She just finished reading *The
Silence of the Lambs* by Thomas Harris; sitcoms and cartoons
can't even come *close*, in interest, to Hannibal the Cannibal
(the mad psychiatrist in *Silence*).

So if your son is pre–high school age and reading a lot,
be pretty casual about the television watching. Reading will
win. Let your daughter spend time watching dumb sitcoms.
She'll get tired of them and then will be much more com-
mitted to choosing books over television if *she's* the one who
makes the decision.

But suppose your children are like the average children
in this country, reading only a few minutes a day and watching hours of television. What do you do?

Do All the Other Things to Encourage Reading That I've Suggested

I think many children choose television over books simply because television is *there*, and one can't fail at watching
television. My students who reported reading little as young
children rarely reported television watching as the reason.
The comment by this sixteen-year-old girl was typical:
"The reason for my dislike of reading was that I have always
been a slow reader, and when I was young, teachers did not

put me in the higher reading group. This made me feel stupid, and I was discouraged. This lowering of self-esteem is part of the reason why I didn't read very much, not because of TV being a distraction."

So it seems to me, with a daughter like this, you double your efforts to make reading a successful experience for her. Find comics she can read. Find easy series books. Praise her reading. Treat her like a reading expert with the books she is reading. Help reading to become a pleasure for her, and it will compete successfully with television.

One student spent a great deal of time for me describing how her parents encouraged her to read: "The positive feeling I got from this developed my desire to read, and it also encouraged good behavior and a stronger parent-child relationship. Most young children want to watch TV because they feel that their parents don't want them to do it. I didn't care about TV."

Again and again, my students commented on how parents could lure children away from television by providing them with many books, and by reading to them. "Probably the greatest influence on my reading was and is my mother, who gave her love of reading to me. This is something I will cherish and enjoy the rest of my life."

So if you have a child who isn't reading but is watching great quantities of television, focus mainly on doing all the things I have suggested to help develop a love of reading. Spend most of your time and energy encouraging reading. But to cover your bases, you might, very quietly and casually, discourage television as well.

How?

Wage a Little Guerrilla Warfare

There are a number of things you can do to discourage television watching and encourage reading without setting up elaborate rules. I'd suggest you have only one television, to start with. Have the television in the living room or den, so that if your son is grouchy and wants privacy, he'll have to go elsewhere, away from the television.

Never have a television in the kitchen. Have a bookcase there instead, and make sure it is filled with comics, magazines, local newspapers, etc. Put out the word that all snacks have to be eaten in the kitchen. Don't explain that this is so your daughter will read while she snacks—we're being sneaky and noncontrolling, remember? Just say that you saw mice in the den, or that crumbs are ruining the carpet, or you're tired of having ants crawl all over the couch. (Import some, if necessary.) Since it's a scientific fact that the average teenage boy can only go eight minutes without putting food in his mouth, your teen should get a lot of reading done if he reads while he's snacking.

And you would never, ever, *dream* of putting a television set in your son's or daughter's bedroom! You want your kids to fall asleep over books, not glued to a flickering screen. Almost all my avid readers report reading themselves to sleep. So their bedrooms should have lots of books and comics—and *no* television!

Should you get cable TV? I think that's sort of a judgment call. On the one hand, you could get basic cable and a sports channel—and with any luck an adult in the house will usurp the television on a regular basis to watch hockey games and tennis matches. You certainly don't want to get a cable service that brings all kinds of shows your kids will love into the house. Who needs that much more competition? Tell your kids you can't afford cable. You're saving for their college tuition. Or you can handle cable the way I did when we moved. I called the cable company.

"I know exactly what I want, basic cable and the sports channel. Just hook it up and send me the bill."

"I'm sorry, ma'am, but we need to come out for a personal interview."

"No, I don't have time. And I know exactly what I want."
"But our policy is that we need a personal interview before . . . "
"Let me talk to your supervisor."
Well, the supervisor gave me the same story so I finally
said, "Fine, we won't get any cable." And we didn't. Now
my kids still tell everyone that we don't have cable because
their mother got in a fight with the cable company.

But what if all this still doesn't work? You've got magazines and comics all over the house. You're very adroitly
discouraging television. And your son *still* spends hours and
hours a day glued to that screen—and never picks up any
reading material at all. Your daughter doesn't even glance
at the *Seventeen* magazine on the coffee table. Her *Soccer
World* sits unread while she watches TV sports all day. What
do you do?

Try Drastic Measures If There Continues to Be No Reading and Great Amounts of TV Watching

If my child was getting to around twelve or thirteen years
old, and was still completely uninterested in reading anything, and was still completely hooked on television, I'd do
something drastic. What do you have to lose? If your kid
continues this way, he'll end up, at best, semiliterate. Almost all professional occupations will be closed to him.
Even jobs in trade will be difficult. How can you repair a
refrigerator if you can't read the directions manual?

What can you do? You might just get rid of your television, to start with. I know that's drastic, but the situation is
drastic. And I know that your son will still watch some
television at a neighbor's house, but at least he won't be
watching at home. And maybe, sooner or later, he'll be
bored enough to pick up and start leafing though some of

the reading material you've been getting him. It's probably better to get rid of TV altogether rather than try to impose heavy restrictions and turn into the Fascist TV Police.

You also should consider getting him into some kind of situation—like a summer camp, or a long family camping trip—where he'll be completely away from any entertainment except for reading. My husband told me that sailors are famous for doing a lot of reading while they're at sea. There's nothing else to do when they're off duty. My son really started reading a lot the summer we took an extended trip through Europe. On the long plane, car, and train rides there wasn't anything else to do.

So be creative! Rent a cabin by a lake for the summer, and bring no television with you. Make sure the nearest town, and movie theatre, is miles away. Bring lots of reading material!

I really think that once you break that initial lock on television—and your son sees there's a whole exciting world out there in books and magazines—he won't ever go back to that television stupor state.

Of course, it would be wonderful if you never had to go through all this worry and planning about television and reading. It would be wonderful if your child had read early and well—and had never felt like a failure at reading, and so had never stopped reading. If you still have a preschooler at home, a good way to ensure that this failure cycle never starts is to teach that preschooler to read. I explain how in the next chapter.

8

PRESCHOOLERS

ANOTHER QUIZ!

The best way to prepare a three- or four-year-old to be a good reader in elementary school is to:

A. Enroll your preschooler in a classy preschool program where he'll make all of the right connections for life.
B. Read to your preschooler all the time.
C. Read to your preschooler a lot but also teach him how to read for himself.

I was never tempted by A. Who wants their child's playmates to arrive in a limo? But a few years ago I would have chosen B, without a doubt. I believed all the educational experts when they said that the best preparation a child could have for reading was a love of books nurtured by many read-aloud sessions. Actually, I guess I still believe that. Reading aloud to your young children is crucial.

The difference is that now I've had the experience of a child that I bought books for, read aloud to, took to the library—and then watched struggle with reading all through

114

elementary school, always being in the lowest reading group.

One of my younger sisters, Nancy, was in the lowest reading group in first grade. She described the experience to me once.

"It was awful. I used to close my eyes and pretend to be in the bathroom when Sister Terence called our group. I thought if I wished hard enough I could be there. I didn't want to be in the reading group because I never knew what was going on."

She recovered by second grade and made it to the highest group, but that's an unusual accomplishment. It took my son Tim until high school to really recover. And one of the things I feel saddest about is that I could have so easily taught him to read before he ever started school. I taught his older sister, Julie. She was born with a cleft palate, which meant she suffered frequent hearing losses because her eustachian tubes didn't drain properly. I taught her to read because I hoped it would help her speech. If she had a visual picture of the words, I figured, the intermittent hearing losses wouldn't matter so much. (I realized how much of a problem she had when all her four-year-old friends came to me one day to see if they, also, could go to beach lessons twice a week. Actually, Julie was going to *speech* lessons, but with her poor articulation, it somehow came out "beach lessons." The whole neighborhood was green with envy.)

But Tim heard perfectly, loved books, and had a large, sophisticated speaking vocabulary. So it never occurred to me that he would have a problem learning how to read. He was the sort of kid who should have picked up reading with the ease that he had picked up oral language. But he didn't. He read almost nothing until third grade and didn't become a really fluent, enthusiastic reader until high school.

Why do I think I could have taught him when the schools couldn't? Maybe I wouldn't have been successful, either—but I certainly wish I'd given it a try. I think it's very easy for a kid to get overlooked in school—and Tim was kind of an unassuming kid—and I know personal attention is the key for anyone who is having an especially hard time learning a skill.

The really dumb thing is that I still hadn't gotten the message when my youngest, Molly, was in preschool. Again, I read to her, bought her books, did everything the reading experts said to do. But I didn't teach her to read. She was another kid who seemed to have everything going for her—very bright, very verbal, very interested in everything. Her birthday was in November, but her preschool teachers told me to start her in first grade at five and a half, rather than kindergarten. She knew her alphabet, colors, shapes, everything a kid is supposed to know before learning to read in first grade.

So I did, and after a few weeks I called her teacher to ask how she was doing. She was doing fine, although she was a little young, the teacher assured me. Of course, she was in all the lowest groups, but she was doing well in them.

Forget that, I said, and pulled her out and put her in kindergarten. I *still* didn't really think to teach her how to read, but luckily, she pretty much taught herself. So, like my older daughter, she was able to go through elementary school in the highest reading groups. School was a lot more pleasant for her, and for her older sister, than for my son.

So that's why I think you should teach your preschooler to read. Don't risk him not learning easily in school. Try to ensure that he doesn't have to endure the stigma and sadness of being one of the "dumb" kids.

And if you follow the principles for enjoyable activities that I mention in the game plan chapter, the experience can be a fun, positive one for both of you. Remember to always make the activities easy, interesting, and engrossing for your child, and to treat him like an expert. Then even if you don't get him to the point where he is fluently reading, he's had fun doing special things with you—and he's probably learned enough about the letters and sounds that he'll pick up reading easily in school. At any rate, as long as you keep it easy and fun, I don't see what you have to lose. And if you can ensure that your child enters school as one of the "smart" kids—well, that's worth a little extra effort, isn't it?

So here's my advice on how to teach your child to read. It's how I taught my older daughter to read—and how I *wish* I'd taught my two other children.

Teach Letters First

There are all kinds of ways to do this. Read alphabet books. They're great. My kids loved the Richard Scarry and the I Can Read books. You can also stick magnetic letters on the refrigerator. Draw letters on pads of papers while you're waiting with your son to see the doctor.

The trick in all this is never to quiz your child. Kids hate to be quizzed. Think about how he learned the rest of his vocabulary. You didn't go around saying, "What's that? Yes! Good! That's a chair!" No, you just used terms naturally in your speech, and he picked it up. So do the same thing with the letters.

"There's a letter B!" you say excitedly, when it drops off the refrigerator onto the floor *again*. "Oh, don't throw that H at your sister!"

If you want to see if anything's sticking, or you just want to have some more fun-with-letters-time, you can start making mistakes. Call the C letter a Q, and see if he notices. Play dumb. "You mean that's really a C?" You're letting him be the expert here, *and* letting him correct his parent—always a very pleasurable activity for any child.

Never make a big deal of this letter teaching. Do it very casually. Actually, the best tool for teaching letters may be *Sesame Street.* It's a wonderful show, one I enjoyed as much as my kids—and they have some really fun skits and songs for teaching letters.

So you're teaching letters, and as soon as this is going well you can branch out to sounds.

Teach the Initial Sounds of the Most Commonly Used Letters

Phonics is often presented as a very complicated subject. But it doesn't have to be. You're not going to get into triple consonant blends. If you can get your child to connect the initial sounds of letters with the letter, your child can start reading. Actually, my own private theory is that that's all of the formal phonics a child ever needs to learn. They pick up the rest when they start reading widely. Needless to say, there are many workbook publishers and remedial reading experts who are not in agreement with me.

But nevertheless, the initial sounds are fine for a start. Again, teach them very casually. "I think I'll have something for lunch that starts with an S. Maybe a sandwich. Do you want a sandwich too?"

If your child just wants some bologna, you can say excitedly, "Oh, you want a B word for lunch!"

Obviously, you don't want to overdo this. And as your child starts catching on, you want to start playing dumb, so he can have more fun.

"I think I'll have a w word for dessert. I'm going to have a cookie. Cookie starts with w!"

I'm sure you get the idea. You can play games when your child is really getting the hang of it—who can find the most things that start with R? Of course, make sure you lose 90 percent of the time. Keep it light and keep it fun.

I think I'd start with the letter recognition when your child is about three, and the initial sounds at around three and a half or four. A lot depends on your own child, of course. Some children pick up on this stuff earlier, some later. But give it a try. If you keep it light and fun, it can't hurt.

After your child has the initial sounds down, you can start teaching him some words.

How to Teach Word Recognition

Again, fun and easy are your operative words. No quizzing. Your child is the expert. Here are a few things I used to do with Julie.

I used to write words on index cards and tape them to the things they named, like chair, piano, and, of course, Julie. (Tim was just a baby then, and Julie was not pleased that he kept pulling the BABY tag off.) You can elaborate on this game by just tagging one or two things, and then letting your child direct you to the proper object on which to place the tag.

When I'd take Julie shopping I'd write out a list. The earliest list had two words on it: *bank* and *store*. She crossed off *bank* and then *store* as we made our rounds. Then I started adding words like *eggs*, *milk*, and *butter*. Pretty soon she was handling ten or more words, and one of my fondest memories of her is watching her sit in the middle of the aisle of the very busy Fort Ord Commissary in California, crossing off words.

Then we moved on to books. When I'd read to her I'd ask her to tell me her favorite word in the story. That was her word, and whenever I came to that word I'd stop, and she'd say it. Pretty soon we were up to two words, three, and more. You have to be careful here, though. Sometimes your child won't want to play this game. Sometimes he'll just want to hear the story, and of course that's fine. Remember, fun and easy.

To help Julie learn the little words that you can't picture, like *if* and *but* and *when*, I invented a game called Reading Fish. I'd write each word on two index cards, and then we'd play fish. I'd pull one of my cards, lay it down where she could see it, and say, "Do you have a *when* like this one?"

When she'd lay down a card I'd say, "Oh, a *that!* Let's see, do I have a *that?*"

Again, only do this game as long as it's fun. In the beginning you'll want to add any words your child already knows and just gradually work in the harder words. But always tell your child what the word is. And remember: no quizzing!

Another thing I used to do with Julie, when she was about four, was write silly three- and four-word stories—stories like this: *Cat sat. Cat sat on rat. Rat sat on cat! Hat! Rat ate hat.*

I'd read the connecting words, like *on* and *ate*, and Julie would read the other words. She thought it was great fun. Sometimes she'd illustrate the stories.

When her sight vocabulary was approaching around twenty words, I started scouring the bookstores for very, very easy books. There was a series then called Bright and Early Readers, and one of those books Julie could read. She was so excited! She read it over and over again, to anyone who would listen. And from then on there was no stopping her. She read all of the very easy readers. I was continually searching bookstores and libraries for easy books. Finally I hit on *Dennis the Menace* comics, which are written on about a second-grade level. From there she went to *Richie Rich* comics, and these became the love of her childhood. We probably have about six hundred *Richie Rich* comics in our attic now.

But as you can see, it's not hard to teach a child how to read. It's really pretty easy. And it certainly didn't hurt my relationship with Julie. If anything, it made us closer. But you've just got to remember the operative words: fun and easy.

Sooner or later, of course, all preschoolers grow up and are ready for school. How do you choose a school that will be reading-friendly to your child? Read on to see.

9

A READING-FRIENDLY SCHOOL

IF YOU'RE IN THE POSITION OF BEING ABLE TO CHOOSE A school system for your children—if you're contemplating a move, or are able to afford private schools—take some time to make the best choice. Just because no school systems (that I've ever seen) are *wonderful* at inculcating a love of reading, it doesn't mean that some aren't clearly better than others. Obviously, if you can find a school system that is set up with much independent, student-choice reading at all levels, in all subjects, go for that school system! But I'm not sure those systems exist.

So look for other things. You want your child to be in a school where he can happily learn. And although you're going to be doing much at home to make sure your child loves reading, it will help if the school system is at least reading-friendly—and friendly to learning in general. So here's the kind of school I want for my own children.

The heart of your child's experience in school takes place in the classroom, specifically in the interaction among the students and between the students and teacher. I would make a real effort to get inside as many classrooms as I could before choosing a school. Look for these things:

A Teacher Who Truly Likes and Enjoys Her Students

I'm convinced that this is the most critical factor in providing a happy school experience for children. A warm, loving teacher will reach out to your child and make him comfortable with the other students and with himself. Most important, there is less chance that a teacher who truly cares about your child will make that child do meaningless busywork. There is more of a chance that a teacher like this will have the courage to say, "This reader isn't working for John. Let's find something else he'll enjoy reading." Teachers who really care about kids are less likely to sell them down the river to maintain their own image as tough and in control. Teachers who really care about kids want to do well by them.

Through all of my years of undergraduate and graduate work, this was the one element of teaching that I never heard mentioned. The "L" word. You've got to love your kids. That was *never* mentioned. What *was* said, over and over again, was that you shouldn't worry about whether or not kids liked you. There was something very unprofessional, supposedly, about caring if students liked you as a teacher. And supposedly, caring whether or not kids liked you would lead you to make many mistakes as a teacher. You might be too nice to kids. You might not maintain discipline well.

It didn't take me more than a few months in my first year of teaching to realize that the whole question of whether or not students like a teacher is moot. The *critical* factor is that the teacher must communicate to her students that *she* likes *them*. Once I had that figured out, classroom discipline became pretty easy. When a kid misbehaved, I'd just say, "It's a good thing I like you," or "It's a good thing you're such a cute kid." The miscreant would inevitably smile and promise to do better. Once I had a very twitchy, jump-around kind of kid in my class. One day we had a visitor in the classroom. Usually kids are better with visitors, but not this boy. The visitor didn't cramp his style at all, and he was pretty obnoxious. I was losing patience fast, so I pulled him aside after the visitor left. "David," I said, "it's so *unlike* you to be disruptive in class. Is something wrong?" A look of confusion passed over his face. Unlike him? He'd never heard that before. But the idea did wonders for him, and his behavior was light-years better after that. The next year, when I was asked to allow him back into my class, I didn't hesitate at all. I was glad to have him. He was fine. A little warmth and praise had worked wonders.

It was only because of a class of twelve boys in a military school in Virginia that I had grown to care about very much that I started really opening up my curriculum. These were a bunch of really needy ninth-graders, many of whom had been put into military school because their parents found them so hard to deal with at home. My son was two at the time, and I quickly found out that I needed to treat this class much as I treated my two-year-old. I gave them lots of praise, lots of individual attention. As a result, after a few months they felt close to me and really tried to please me.

But reading wasn't going well. We had a large anthology to get through, and they were not enthusiastic about the selections. I finally tested them individually in reading and found that they averaged about a sixth-grade level. No wonder they were having trouble. I talked to the academic dean and asked if I could order some paperbacks for this class. "No, boys don't like to read anyway," he told me—meaning, I guess, that therefore it didn't matter what reading material I gave them. But I really cared about these boys, and one day, while they were struggling through a selection from Carl Sandburg's biography of Lincoln, a fragment of a

popular song ran through my head: "I can't give any more
of my soul away/And still look myself in the mirror every
day." It was probably a love song—I can't remember any
more from it—but it galvanized me. I really cared about
these kids. They couldn't *read*. Time was wasting! "Put
down your books," I told them. "We're going to the library." At the library, with the help of a wonderful librarian,
they all picked out individual reading choices. And that was
it. I never looked back. Soon they were happily reading, I
was hearing about all the good books they had found, and
I resolved never again to make students follow a curriculum
that was not right for them.

But it was only because of the close relationship I had
with that class that I had the courage to do that. So look for
a school with teachers who really are crazy about kids. It's
the factor of overriding importance.

Some schools have a culture that really supports caring
about students. Two of my children were lucky enough to
attend an alternative-elementary school in Acton, Massachusetts, called McCarthy-Towne. It was an incredibly
warm, nurturing place, and I don't think it was any coincidence that the school used regular children's books to teach
reading long before the "whole language" method became
fashionable.

The Catholic high school I taught at in Norfolk, Virginia
was also very warm and student-friendly. The heart of the
school was an advisor system that virtually everyone, from
the principal to the custodian, participated in. Students
chose advisors and usually stayed with that advisor for three
or four years. Again, I think it was no coincidence that it
was at this very nurturing school that I was encouraged to
set up the saturation reading program I wrote about in chapter 1. At this school, a whole staff of caring people made it
work. One young man, who was doing very little reading for
me, had the custodian as an advisor. The custodian would
check with me to see what his advisee should be doing for

English (answer: reading!), and then set the young man down in the boiler room, during all his free periods, with his books. He was like a father to the boy.

So make caring teachers your number-one priority—no matter what level your child is reading on, or what kind of student he is. There is more of a chance that a caring teacher will give an advanced student the freedom and confidence to surge ahead into independent work, and *much* more of a chance that a caring teacher will coax and cajole a poor student into performing. Everyone who has told you that structure, or high expectations, or strict discipline is the most important element is simply wrong. Look for teachers who care about kids.

What kind of school tends to nurture teachers who care about kids?

Look for Low Student-Teacher Ratios and Reasonable Class Loads

Generally, teachers who are treated well themselves have more time and emotional energy to give to kids. So look for small classes in elementary schools and low teacher-student ratios in junior highs and high schools. An elementary class of more than twenty-two or twenty-three students is large, and a high school teacher who teaches more than a hundred kids every day is not going to have much time for individually helping students.

Equally important at the junior high and high school level is the number of classes a teacher is assigned. Most schools assign five classes a day, and that is simply too much. After you teach five classes, and take a duty period, you have about forty minutes left in your day to do all your planning, grading, contacting parents, seeing kids individually, etc. Obviously, that's absurd. Plus you're so tired after teaching five classes that all you can think about is making a cup of tea and perhaps getting some quiz grades recorded. Virtually all your planning and grading gets taken home to do at night, when you're tired and busy with family duties. And there's almost no time to see kids individually.

I've taught as many as seven classes a day, with a student load of 142, and as few as four classes with a student load of 90. There's no comparison. With 143 kids and seven classes, I was lucky if I remembered everyone's name. With four classes and 90 kids, I have the time and energy to help kids with individual and group projects, to assign a good deal of writing, to do independent study projects with students, to talk to parents, even to talk to my colleagues occasionally.

One of my colleagues was describing to me the school in Texas she used to teach in. She had five classes every day, with about 30 kids in each class. That's 150 kids. She said she gave *no* writing assignments—none of the teachers did—because they just didn't have the time or energy to grade them. And allow kids to choose individual books— never mind having the time or knowledge about each kid to help them with the choices—well, that was just laughable. All the students read the same books and were given multiple-choice tests after they were finished.

I've never taught elementary school, but my colleagues assure me the situation is the same there. A teacher who has a large number of students to begin with and then is with them virtually all day has very little time or energy to individualize reading programs, to create new materials or academic units, to talk to parents—to do any of the activities that distinguish an exciting, memorable teacher from a tired, grouchy one who just gets through the day.

I'm a fanatic believer that the best education dollar is not spent on elaborate computer labs, sophisticated in-service programs with outside experts coming in, countless supervisors and other educational bureaucrats. The best education dollar is spent on low teacher-student ratios and reasonable class loads.

Look for a School That Encourages Diverse Styles of Teaching

Just walking down the hallway of a school and glancing into the classrooms can tell you a lot about the comfort level of the teachers there and how free they feel to try new things. Ideally, you should see many different styles of teaching. Some teachers will be standing in front of the class, lecturing or leading discussions—and some teachers do this very well. In some classrooms students will be working in groups, and the teacher will be circulating around the room, offering help here and there. Some classrooms will have students in front of the room, teaching or making reports. In some classrooms the desks will be in a circle to facilitate good class discussions. If you've really found a wonderful school, you might even see a classroom or two where students are lounging comfortably at their desks, reading books of their own choice.

If all of the teachers are lecturing, or doing cooperative learning, or leading discussions, then you probably have a school system with administrators who are too intrusive. Teachers have different strengths and weaknesses, and a school system that respects that will more likely respect the strengths and weaknesses of its students. Teachers are all different, and kids are all different. A system that recognizes and respects that is a good school system for your child.

Another thought:

Look for a School System with Good Counseling Services

I know that some systems are seeing this as a luxury now, but competent counselors and social workers on site are very important. For one thing, many students who are experiencing failure or trauma somewhere in their lives will only agree to get help if the help is familiar and available on a drop-in basis. If the social worker or counselor is part of the school staff, and already a familiar figure in the halls and lunchroom, kids feel much more comfortable agreeing, finally, to talk about their problems. Plus they probably have friends who visit the counselor. He's not an unknown quantity.

You may think now that your children won't ever need the help of a good counselor, and maybe you're right. But circumstances change, families change, kids change. And especially if your son or daughter has been experiencing much failure at school because of a reading disability, it would help to know your child's school has good psychological support services.

The other reason I'd look for good counseling services is because they are a sign that the school system recognizes that kids' emotional needs are important. Good counselors can intercede with teachers and help smooth over rough times for your child. A good counselor can provide the kind of adult emotional support that many teenagers find hard to accept from parents. And of course, good counselors are essential for helping kids weave through the morass of college applications.

There's one final thing to look for, if you're in the position of choosing a school. This is probably the most controversial of all my recommendations. I've mentioned the issue before in passing, but it's important enough to spend a bit of time on. The issue? Ability grouping of students.

Look for a School That Does Very Little Ability Grouping of Students

There's a term that psychologists use, "counterintuitive," which describes a situation where the reality is counter to what we would expect. The classic example is the situation of a battered wife. Common sense would suggest that a woman would be quick to leave an abusive husband; at least we would expect her to seek help. Yet we understand now that the reality is that women often stay in these relationships for years—for very complex social and psychological reasons. This is a counterintuitive situation.

I think ability grouping falls into the same category. It seems to make so much sense: put kids into groups, or classes, with other students of the same ability. Then the work won't be too easy or too hard; it will be work they can comfortably accomplish. They'll gain self-confidence and good academic skills. What could be more obvious?

Unfortunately, it really doesn't work. Carl Glickman, in the May 1991 issue of *Educational Leadership,* summarizes several recent studies when he writes:

> We know that the evidence shows no benefits are gained by tracking students into ability groups, as shown by Oakes (1985), Slavin (1987, 1990), George (1987), and Garmoran and Berends (1987). Higher-achieving students do not do better when together, and lower-achieving students do much worse when together . . . Once assigned to a low track, very few move into higher tracks; and their performance as low achievers becomes self-perpetuating.

First let's talk about low achievers, because I think the fact that low-achieving students do poorly when all together is more easily understood. I've taught many lower-level classes in my twenty years of teaching, probably more than the average teacher because I was frequently the new teacher in a school, and new teachers tend to get the classes no one else wants. Also, after I picked up a degree in learning disabilities, I was a natural for low-level classes.

I'm pretty good with these classes—I really care about

the kids, I know how to run individualized reading and writing programs—but I'm not good *enough*. And I don't know anyone who is good enough.

There's a sense of malaise that permeates low-level classes. Kids have been told, in effect, that they are not as good as other students. It's no surprise that, by high school, they believe it. I think there's almost a class depression that sets in. In addition, these classes are often heavily weighted with students with serious personal problems. A class can absorb a couple of kids with problems—the teacher can make extra time for them, and they are reluctant to act disruptively in a class where the vast majority of students are well behaved—but when half or more of the students are troubled, the class becomes almost unteachable.

Another problem, as I've mentioned before, is that students who are always in low-level classes have no idea of the kind of academic performance possible when students are really working hard. I've noted that poor readers have no idea, until they're in a mixed class, that it's possible to read a whole book in a day or two—until they hear their classmates reporting doing just that. For a lot of kids, a sense of competition will kick in, and all of a sudden they're spending many more hours a week reading, trying to keep up with their friends.

Implicit in this discussion of low-level classes, of course, is my solid belief that, by high school anyway, "ability" leveling has little or nothing to do with the innate ability of students; rather, it has everything to do with their level of motivation, and their level of intelligence developed over years of reading or not reading, thinking critically or not thinking critically, etc. I don't say this lightly. Twenty years of teaching have completely convinced me of this. There certainly is a difference in performance level by high school. But I've only had a handful of students, over the last twenty years, who seemed to me to be truly lacking in innate intelligence.

When the research showing the deleterious effect of tracking began surfacing in the mideighties, I was really relieved. I always had the idea, in the back of my mind, that if I just tried hard enough, I could get the same enthusiastic level of learning from my low-level classes as I got from the higher-level classes. It was a relief to know that maybe the problem wasn't with me; maybe the kids and I were in a no-win situation—maybe the problem was tracking.

But of course, advocates of tracking have never loudly extolled its virtues for kids in low levels. Few parents storm the placement offices of high schools demanding that their son or daughter be placed in remedial English. No, the advocates of tracking focus almost entirely on the necessity of having "demanding, rigorous courses" for students who are more adept at the academic game. It's the kids in high-level courses that everyone worries about.

So let's talk about them. I did an interesting experiment a couple of years ago. We don't formally level upper-class English courses at my high school—any student can sign up for any course—but some courses are harder than others. I was teaching a course in British literature—one of our harder electives. Some of my students had been complaining because neither the English nor the social studies departments had any honors or advanced placement courses. (We have a lot of good courses; we just don't like leveling, labeling, and restricting access to them.) The science and math departments, on the other hand, have four levels of courses: honors, enriched, level one, and level two. Almost all of my British literature class reported being in either honors or enriched science classes. So I asked them one day, apropos of nothing, if, over the last three years—the class was mostly juniors—they had found their science courses or their social studies courses to be more "exciting, challenging, and thought provoking." I passed out little slips of paper and told them to vote anonymously.

The social studies courses won, hands down. It wasn't

even close. My class was floored when I pointed out that, even though they said they wanted honors courses in social studies, they found their mixed classes more "exciting, challenging, and thought provoking" than their honors courses in science.

The results were so interesting that we forgot about British literature for a day and discussed the survey results. Why did they find their science courses less exciting and demanding than their social studies courses? At first they said that perhaps the social studies teachers were better, but I gently reminded them that, on an earlier, school-wide survey for a different purpose, they had named both social studies and science as departments with particularly good teachers. They thought about that for a minute, and then agreed. So what was the difference?

A few kids suggested that, in their honors science and math classes, newer concepts and theories weren't taught very thoroughly. The teachers just assumed the students would understand the concepts without a lot of teaching. A lot of heads in the class nodded. In social studies classes, with everyone from the school clown to the class valedictorian, teachers didn't dare assume anything, and everything was thoroughly taught. Also, of course, they noted that in social studies classes they were often given more choice on projects and readings. Again, of course, in a mixed class, a teacher has to give more choice.

Even in this group of high-achieving students, there was poignant testimony about the deleterious effects of tracking. One excellent student remarked that, in seventh grade, she was not allowed to take honors math because there weren't enough chairs in the room. "So I never could get into honors math," she told us, "because I was always behind. And now, when someone asks me for help on a math problem, I always tell them that I'm not very good in math—they should find someone in the honors section."

If this student, who was in top courses in every other field,

had her self-confidence lowered because of her math placement in an *enriched* course, imagine how students who are
routinely slotted into all low-level classes feel.

Since this discussion with my British literature class, I've
thought a lot about tracking and realized some other things.
My sister mentioned that perhaps top students got more
attention in a mixed class. I thought about that and realized
that she was absolutely right. In a mixed class top students
are special. When I only have a few in a class I do pay special
attention, often reading books along with them, making
them be group leaders in discussion groups, talking to them
seriously about how the course is going. Of course, we often
draft the top students to help their less academically successful classmates, but I think this is good too. The best
way to learn something is to teach it. It also assures that
these top students will be able to work with the great di-
versity of people they'll meet in future job situations.

And I've realized something else about mixed classes. I
think maybe my class's first reaction—that the social studies
teachers were better—was based on the recognition that the
social studies teachers are, on the whole, the most colorful
teachers in the school. There are the highest percentage of
"characters" in the social studies department. But I think
that this too is perhaps a result of their having only mixed
classes. One needs to be a bit of a showman to keep the
interest of a mixed group of kids.

I thought back to what was probably the worst class I've
ever observed. It was an honors sophomore English class,
in a neighboring town. This class was the highest of four
levels, and it was obvious that all the students in this class
were docile, hardworking, ready-to-play-the-academic-
game type of kids. The teacher spent the entire period
droning on about a very boring essay in their literature anthology. The kids all dutifully took notes. I could hardly
stay awake.

A teacher in a mixed class would never get away with this

kind of teaching. The more active, less academic kids would be swinging from the fluorescent lights in ten minutes—or less. A mixed class simply demands that a teacher be a more creative, interesting, innovative teacher.

Having said all this, I guess I do need to point out that the higher up the academic ladder a student travels, the less possible, in some subjects, mixed classes become. You really can't put a student who can't do long division into calculus. But a school *can* allow any student to *try* any class, and a school can provide the kind of support necessary for a student weak in a subject to try a more difficult class. At my school, for example, the math, English, and social studies departments have resource centers which are open all day to any student in the school. A teacher and usually a tutor staff the centers at all times. Students can go to these centers for extra help or just to make up any tests or quizzes they've missed. I think centers like these really help to eliminate the need for rigid tracking.

So there you have my tips for choosing a reading-friendly school. Look for warm teachers, reasonable teaching loads, a variety of teaching styles, good counseling services, and as little academic tracking as possible. Of course, other things are important too. Bright, warm, clean buildings send a message that the morale and health of students and teachers is valued. A well-stocked library shows the school supports literacy. A good athletic program builds self-esteem in kids. Well-supported music and art programs develop talents that will give students pleasure their whole life. Friendly, smiling faces in the hallway—on administrators, teachers, and kids—show the school is a caring, kid-friendly place.

So when choosing a school for your children, choose a school for the right reasons. Forget status and reputation: find a school where your child can happily learn.

One caveat: what you can't do very often is decide to change your child's school. It takes a long time, at least a year is my guess, for children to feel comfortable in a new school. Unless the new school is absolutely wonderful, and unless your child is willing to make the change, I'd be very cautious. If the school your child is in is okay—not wonderful, but okay—and he is doing all right, and doesn't want to move, I wouldn't move him unless I absolutely had to. Trust me on this. I've seen more kids, especially as they approach the vulnerable teen years, absolutely devastated by a move.

But let's assume that you have your child happily settled in the best school you can manage. Problems will still arise. No school is perfect; no child is perfect. How do you handle common school problems?

Read on!

10

COMMON SCHOOL PROBLEMS

WHAT DO YOU DO WHEN YOUR SIXTH-GRADER COMES home and reports that all his reading teacher does is make the class memorize vocabulary and do reading-skill cards? What do you do when your ninth-grader is put into the lowest level of English classes? What do you do when your tenth-grader is assigned to read a book that he simply can't get through?

There are few things harder for parents to do than to watch their child struggle unhappily and unprofitably in school. I certainly don't have all the answers, but over the years, both as a parent and as a teacher, I've developed a philosophy for handling such problems. I think it helps to think out ahead of time—before the heat of the immediate situation—your reaction to problems.

Have Clear Priorities

I suggest that even more important than having children become avid readers is having children grow up to be self-confident, independent adults. I think we want our children to be able to handle problems with courage and humor. We want our children to grow into adults who find joy in work and in personal relationships.

Now, I don't think anyone has figured out exactly how to produce children like this, but I do know a common ingredient in these wonderful kids is a strong sense of self-esteem. And I know at least two conditions necessary to produce this self-esteem: children need to be loved unconditionally, and children need the chance, and the encouragement, to experience success in a number of different areas of their lives.

Much has been written about loving children unconditionally, and I don't think I can add anything to the discussion—but I do think the issue of children achieving success is not as clear.

Remember when your daughter first started dressing herself? Remember the great combinations—the plaid skirt, the striped shirt, the flowered tights? You told her she looked wonderful, because the joy and self-confidence she gained from dressing herself were more important than having her look like a mini fashion model. The best picture I have of my younger daughter was taken at school when she was about ten. She had on an old T-shirt that her brother had tie-dyed for her, and an even older sweater of mine that was falling off her shoulders.

"I forgot they were going to take pictures today," she confided to me after school, as my eyes were widening at her ragamuffin appearance, "but *luckily* I had on my favorite outfit!"

And the picture that later arrived home in her book bag was breathtaking. She is wearing an absolutely radiant smile, because *she* had chosen her outfit and was sure she looked her very best. The viewer doesn't even notice the clothes. The smile lights up the whole photograph—the whole room!

Clearly, that day, her "bad" decision about what to wear was much better for her than my "good" decision would have been. Every parent is familiar with this dilemma. It's snowing out and your fourteen-year-old wants to wear his sneakers. You let him, because a parent making a fourteen-year-old wear boots does great harm to his self-confidence, and you figure, hey, he's young; he'll get over pneumonia quickly anyway. And maybe then he'll wear boots! As children get older, they gradually usurp all the decisions we used to make for them: what to eat, who to play with, how to dress, etc. If we don't start letting them make these decisions, our children won't turn into lovely, joyful, self-confident adults.

When I mentioned in class one day that I never forced my children to eat anything they didn't like, my students were horrified. "You spoil your children," they told me. But I don't think so. Since the heart of my message in regard to reading, and most other aspects of our children's lives, is that we need to empower our children to make their own choices, I'm going to take a minute to describe what I see as the difference between spoiling and empowering children.

If a child doesn't like what's served for dinner, and his parent jumps up and cooks him something else, that child is spoiled. I teach my children that if they don't like something on the dinner table, they may politely refuse a serving, eat what they do like, and then excuse themselves. Later, if they're hungry, they can slip back into the kitchen and fix themselves cereal. It's a critical difference. A spoiled child will tell his mother he needs eighty-dollar sneakers, not caring that she is limping around in ten-dollar dime store specials. An empowered child will be told that the family can afford a certain amount of money for his clothing; he can decide how to allocate it. If he wants to blow it all on sneakers, that's his decision. But that's all the money available for a while. And everyone else in the family also has a reasonable amount of money for clothes. It doesn't all go to him.

Spoiled children are the ones who think the world owes them a living. And ironically, they are not usually happy children. They grow up to be restless and dissatisfied; no one can ever do enough for them. They have a very off-putting sense of entitlement but not, I think, very high self-esteem. Everything has always been done for them, while real self-esteem is based on one's own accomplishments. And it's hard to accomplish much when everyone else is always turning somersaults for you.

Protecting Your Child's Self-Esteem in School

How does all this fit into handling problems at school? Well, simply stated, it means that you can't be very intrusive in your child's school life. There are always a number of parents who are much too involved in their children's school careers. They are always on the phone with teachers, asking about homework and making helpful suggestions about what should happen in class. They talk to administrators a lot, demanding that their child's teacher, or level, or guidance counselor, or schedule, or something else, be changed. And now, the newest wrinkle is that they appear with paid advocates, who have put together a long list of special things the school is supposed to do for their child.

If you've read the first part of this book, you know that, at least as far as reading goes, in no way do I think schools are always right. But—and this is a big but—I think parents like this do much more harm to their own children than good.

The kids of these kinds of parents don't usually function well in school. Often they're timid and nervous, sometimes they are angry and sullen, and sometimes they perfect the art of appearing very pleasant but never actually hand in any work. I think the heart of their problem is low self-esteem, caused by parents who have preempted the child's job of being in charge of his own education.

You're probably saying that this is a ridiculous concept—
that a child should be in charge of his own education. But
from the time the child is eight or nine, I don't see it working any other way. I think it is only when a child is empowered to decide most educational issues himself—such as
when he does his homework, what level of math he should
be in, how he should deal with a teacher who is assigning a
book he can't read—that you have a chance of ending up
with an independent, self-confident student.

This doesn't mean that you don't have a role to play. You
have a very important role. You listen to your child, you
validate his insight and his emotions, and you offer your
services to help him.

Listening to Your Child

By far the most valuable educational conference I ever
attended was given by the Dominican nuns in California in
the early 1970s. The Dominican school where I was teaching sent me to a conference in San Francisco. The speaker
at this conference described the concept—very well known
now—of active listening. It simply means that when you
listen to someone, your whole goal is to find out exactly
what that person is thinking and feeling. You don't intrude
your own opinions on the conversation, because that tends
to shut the speaker down. I immediately tried it on my
three-year-old who, up to that time, had been telling me
very little about what was going on in nursery school when
I asked direct questions.

"Julie, I see you were digging with a shovel when I came
to get you."

"Yes." A silence then, but I didn't say anything. Finally:
"It was John's shovel. I hit him over the head with the
bucket to get it."

"Oh." I was quiet for a minute, thinking about this. I

finally came up with, "I guess you like digging with shovels."

"Yes! I have all the shovels. I hide them in the sand."

Well, I'm sure you get the idea. I may finally have worked in the gentle suggestion that maybe she'd have more friends if she *shared* her shovels—I am a parent, after all—but active listening is a wonderful way to get kids talking to you. And she did grow up to be such a nonviolent adult that she actually feeds the squirrel that's broken into her apartment, rather than trapping "Ed," as she calls him.

Suppose your daughter comes home complaining about her English teacher.

"I hate Mr. Jones. He's such a jerk! I did all the reading in *A Separate Peace* last night and still failed the quiz. His questions are ridiculous. I hate English!"

First, what you *don't* say:

Don't say: "You should never call a teacher a jerk!"

Don't say: "I'm calling up that teacher right now. I know you did the reading. I saw you!"

Do say: "It must be pretty discouraging to read the book and then fail the quiz."

She'll probably say something like, "*No* one could have passed that test. You'd have to memorize the book!"

Don't say: "Oh, the test couldn't have been that hard. What were some of the questions?"

Do say: "The questions must have been really hard."

Notice that all you're doing is either repeating in another form the information she's given you or verbalizing how she must be feeling. There's a good chance here that she'll actually tell you some of the questions. And, because you've raised a sensible, trustworthy child, there's a good chance that the questions were unreasonable. What do you do then?

You Can Offer Suggestions and Help, but Your Child Needs to Call the Shots

"Those questions do sound really hard," you tell your daughter. "Do you want me to call the teacher and complain?"

The chances are that this will elicit a horrified "No!" If she says yes, then of course you need to call the teacher and gently inform him that his quizzes are demoralizing your daughter. But if she says no, you might make another offer of help.

"Is there anything you want me to do to help you? Read the book with you, maybe?"

This will probably also draw a "No!" but you've accomplished a lot anyway. You've believed her, you're willing to help her, you've validated her feelings, and you've told her, implicitly, that you're trusting her handling of the problem. There's a good chance that she'll just storm out of the kitchen saying that she's just going to have to spend hours and hours reading tonight—but that probably is the best answer. Either that, or she finds a copy of Cliffs Notes and you pretend not to notice. But at any rate, you have to let her handle it. It's *her* problem. It's her handling small problems like this that gives her the self-confidence and self-esteem to be a well-functioning adult later in life. And *that's* what's most important.

What about When the Problems Are Big?

Having your daughter fail a quiz on a novel is not the end of the world. But what about this scenario? Your son comes home and announces that he has Mrs. Cajon for English, and she's the worst teacher in the school!

"What do you mean, the worst teacher?" you ask.

"*All* you do in class is grammar and vocabulary," he says despairingly, "and she's *mean*. Last year she gave Matt detention because he walked over to the counter during class to get a Kleenex, and she told Sarah that she was a lazy slob because she didn't do her homework when she had mono. She's always yelling at kids. Everyone hates her."

Now I know that the conventional wisdom is that you should tell your child to buck up, life isn't all a bed of roses, and maybe she's really an excellent teacher that kids don't like because she's hard. I probably would have thought that myself, twenty years ago. But since then I've seen enough teachers like this—not many, but enough—to know that what that student is describing is a teacher who emotionally batters students. And I will not have my child in a classroom with a teacher like that. Even if my child asks me not to do anything to get him out—which is rare, because children usually will accept parental help to get them out of a classroom with a teacher they fear—I'd think that the slight loss in self-confidence my child might suffer from my interference would be less than the harm he would suffer from a year-long exposure to an emotionally battering teacher.

This is what I'd do. First I'd try to see if my son's perception was accurate. If he'd had the teacher for a couple of months, I'd trust his assessment. If he'd only had her for a few days, I'd try to confirm his opinion by talking to the teacher, and also by talking to other parents and students who might have had her. Sometimes a teacher will seem very unreasonable the first few days but actually turn out to be just fine. So check around. If it looks as if the teacher might be marginally okay, sit tight. Intruding in your son's education is something you don't want to do very often. Make sure that this is one of the few, very necessary times before you do anything.

And if you do finally determine that this will be a very destructive teacher for your son to have, try to extricate him from her classroom as unobtrusively as possible. Again, this is for the benefit of your son. You don't want to embarrass him or make him a cause célèbre. Tell your son to go first to his guidance counselor. Maybe the counselor can just quietly switch your son's schedule. Maybe the two of them can manufacture a conflict (like your son wanting to switch into music from photography, which will necessitate an English change). If this works, you're golden. Your son has effected the change himself, *and* he's out of that class.

But it might not work. My own son was assigned to an awful math teacher one year (who I knew was awful because my older daughter had already had him). Guidance wouldn't switch him because, as the principal explained to me in an unguarded moment, "If we let everyone switch out of his class who wanted to, there wouldn't be anyone left." Then you have to get tough.

"I want him out," I told the principal. "I don't care what you have to do. Move him up a level, move him down a level, change his whole schedule around, whatever. But I want him out!"

That managed to extricate him. If that tactic doesn't work for you, you could explain gently to the principal that you are very unhappy, and that you're going to ask your child every day what went on in class. You're going to take notes. Maybe you'll send your notes to the school board. Maybe you'll write a letter to the local paper. You don't want to do this—who wants to turn their child into Snitch of the Year?—but you don't see any other option.

I probably wouldn't go this far. If the situation was intolerably bad, and the school would not assign my child another English teacher, I'd simply withdraw him from his English class, give him a study for that period, and plan on having him attend summer school.

You might say, but shouldn't you do something to get rid of that teacher? If she's hurting my child, she's probably hurting other children too. Yes, of course, but my own child always comes first with me. I don't want him caught in the crossfire, if I can help it. That's why you try all the quiet, least intrusive methods first. Later, when your child has safely graduated or moved on, you can be more vocal.

And actually, by refusing to allow your child to stay in that class, you've accomplished a lot. If a good number of parents follow your lead, sooner or later the administrators will find a way to get that teacher out of the classroom. She's just causing too much trouble for them. The last thing educational administrators want is any trouble.

On to more problems!

How to Deal with Tracking

Even though you're going to look for a school with little or no tracking, you probably won't be able to find one. Most schools still do a significant amount of tracking. How do you maneuver your child through this maze?

In elementary school you can't do much. Often, you aren't even informed which reading group your child is in. Since it all takes place in one classroom, with one teacher, you really don't have much say. But at home you'll be doing the things I recommend in the first part of this book, and sooner or later your child's reading will improve to the point that the teacher should notice and move him up. If she doesn't, and your child wants to change groups, have him talk to her. If she won't listen to your son you can, with your son's permission, try yourself. But in an elementary school classroom you don't have much leverage.

Things change in junior high and high school. Different levels are in separate classrooms, and usually your child's current teacher will recommend he continue at the same level for the following year. Unless you are trying to get your child into an honors or gifted section, you can probably do a parental override and move your child up to a level higher than the one recommended. When should you do this?

The rule of thumb is that you want your child in a class where he is challenged but can comfortably do the work. There is a lot of misunderstanding around this issue. The child's intelligence isn't the issue. The skill level and level of motivation are the deciding criteria.

The worst thing to do is to decide that, since your child is intelligent, he should take a course like British literature—even though he isn't much of a reader. If he isn't much of a reader, no matter how bright he is, he's going to have trouble reading Chaucer and John Donne and Jane Austen. And there's no way to tutor him through a class like this. Even if a tutor reads all the required reading aloud to him, he won't have developed the verbal sophistication to really follow it. Verbal sophistication, remember, comes with avid reading. Eventually, if you follow my suggestions, your child will be an avid reader. But if he's not there yet, don't put him in a situation he can't handle.

Even more important than skill level, however, is motivation. In fact, motivation is so important that, even if I was pretty sure my daughter lacked the reading level to understand British literature, if she seriously wanted to take the course and asked me to sign a parental override, I would. Kids can do work they theoretically shouldn't be able to do, if they try hard enough. But you can't assume this level of motivation. And you certainly can't *assign* this level of motivation to your child: "I'm putting you in a very hard course, but I know if you work as hard as you can you'll get through." I can guarantee you that kid won't work as hard as he can. In fact, he may get angry and not work at all.

Finally, if your teenager—your daughter, let's say—is going through a difficult personal time, I think you should encourage her to take courses she can complete without a great deal of effort. If her personal life is in an upheaval, she simply won't have the emotional energy, or ability to concentrate, to do well in demanding academic subjects. If she's in a course that's pretty easy for her, she may get through it all right, and so at least not have to worry about school achievement. When her personal life is sorted out, she can go back to taking more demanding courses.

What If Your Child Is Failing All or Most of His Courses?

Every high school teacher is familiar with this phenomenon: a kid who maybe wasn't doing wonderfully in school, but was at least passing, all of a sudden is failing courses— and not just one course. He's probably cutting classes too, and perhaps getting into an equal amount of trouble outside school. What's going on?

It's tempting, of course, to decide that this teenager—it's usually a teenager—has some undiscovered learning disability that's just shown up. Maybe he can't integrate his auditory and visual memory. Or maybe his poor reading skills have finally caught up with him. Could he just be lazy? Maybe he has a new girlfriend and can think of nothing else.

In my twenty years of teaching, I've never seen one of these possibilities be the cause of massive school failure at a high school level. A huge number of high school students have poor or mediocre reading skills. A learning disability so debilitating as to cause failure across a wide range of subjects would have caused the failure much earlier than high school. I don't think I've ever seen a kid who was simply lazy. There was always much more going on. He was depressed, or angry, or in full-fledged rebellion. And the presence or loss of a girlfriend is only of critical importance if there is a lack somewhere else in the teen's life.

So what does cause this type of massive failure? I hate to sound repetitive, but I do think that a self-esteem problem is virtually always at the bottom of it. A family crisis, such as a divorce, death, remarriage, or illness, can cause this dive in self-esteem, although I'm not sure why. Maybe the kids think they somehow should have prevented the crisis, or should be doing something now to fix it. A long-standing family problem can suddenly, because of all the other stresses of adolescence, become more difficult for the teenager to deal with, a problem such as parental alcoholism, neglect, abuse, overprotection, or overcontrol.

This doesn't mean that I blame the parent who comes to see me because her son is failing. Not at all. A lot of sad things in life just happen, and often the parent I see is the survivor who's tried hard to protect her child from difficult family situations. Unfortunately, this well-meaning parent is often told by the school to do exactly the kinds of things that will lower her son's feeling of worth even further.

For example, the teachers will start calling home, telling the parent about all the homework the son has missed. The message is clear: the parent had better ensure that the child complete this homework. I call this the Tattle Theory of Motivation. It may work for a short time, but it always ultimately results in even further lowering the student's self-esteem, and so lowering, rather than raising, his motivation and performance.

As a teacher, the only thing I've found that works with this kind of student is a lot of personal attention, a lot of manufacturing success—and giving much praise—and a lot of overlooking a less-than-wonderful performance. I had a student one time who, at the age of nineteen, was still trying to finish high school. I had her during the first period in the morning, and she was almost always late. That was okay. I gave her a big smile when she arrived because I really was glad to see her—and I knew how hard it was for her to get herself to school each morning. The other kids did a bit of writing every day; often she couldn't quite bring herself to do that. That was okay. I talked about her books with her, got a bit of writing from her every so often, praised her for being so insightful—she really *was* insightful; she took my breath away sometimes with the things she'd say—and just generally tried to make the class an esteem-enhancing experience for her. After a while I could see her becoming more relaxed. She started arriving on time more often. She started doing the daily writing with the rest of the class. She became a real asset to have in the class because she became more comfortable about speaking up and sharing her wonderful insight.

Now I know this way of handling so-called problem students goes against much conventional wisdom. Kids who fail are supposed to be in very structured environments; reward/punishment systems are supposed to be set up to make them conform to school standards. They get points for coming on time, doing homework assignments according to specifications, etc.

This may work with some kids; I've just never seen it work with any of mine. My problem is that I can so clearly feel the pain of these students—they don't *want* to fail and feel like losers—that I can't do anything but be gentle and encouraging with them. And luckily, I've found that, for me, that works best. My guess is it works because my caring helps build up, a little, the student's shattered self-esteem.

So my advice is that you do anything that will increase your teenager's self-esteem—listening to him, empowering him to make decisions, praising him whenever even remotely possible, helping him to find activities to succeed at—and avoid doing things that lower his self-esteem. Don't ground him. Don't tell him he's a disgrace to the family. Don't forbid him use of the car (unless, of course, there's a substance-abuse problem). Don't call his teachers every other day to check up on him. Don't criticize his friends. Sooner or later, believe me, your efforts will pay off, and you'll see him turn the corner and start believing in himself again.

You also might want to investigate therapy, for your troubled teenager and for the rest of the family. A good therapist can be a big help in getting families through rough times. If your teenager won't go, go yourself. The therapy will help you in dealing with the situation, and it will communicate to your son that you're willing to investigate your own motives and behavior in an effort to help him. Believe me, that's a powerful message for a kid to get.

And certainly, it might help to get some educational testing done. Although I really don't think a slight learning disability ever causes massive school failure, a knowledge of it will help teenagers to feel better about their effort and basic intelligence if they know that some kinds of educational tasks are more difficult for them. For example, I found out in my senior year in high school that I tested in the second percentile for visual memory. Wow! No wonder I couldn't spell and always got lost while I was driving. It helped to know that it wasn't through stupidity that I didn't remember the signposts on a route—Do I turn left at that *yellow* church?—I just had a very poor visual memory. I learned to travel with maps. My computer has a spell-checker.

So do have educational testing done, if it seems warranted, but mostly remember to be gentle and encouraging with your failing son. Build up the self-esteem of your daughter who can't seem to graduate. And of course, be doing all the things I've already talked about to ensure your child will be a lifelong reader. If worse comes to worst, then, and your teen drops out of school and never goes back, he—or she—will still end up better educated than the majority of college graduates!

In the next chapter I discuss school problems specific to poor readers. If your child is still in one of the early reading stages, I think it's important for you to read it.

11

HELPING THE POOR READER COPE WITH SCHOOL

YOUR SON, AT THIS POINT, IS JUST IN THE PAGING-through-magazines stage, or maybe the reading-the-magazines stage. You're buying lots of his favorite periodicals; you're planning the first book to move him toward: it's just a matter of time until his reading really improves. But meanwhile, he's still in school and most likely not doing very well. How do you handle this?

Change Schools?

The school a poor reader attends is vitally important. And even though I advised earlier that you not change your child's school unless you can really help it, you might consider it if these situations exist: all subjects are rigidly leveled; teachers talk much more about "academic excellence" than the individual needs of students; teachers are overworked, with large student loads; the curriculum is rigid and set; and most importantly, your son is unhappy there.

Before you say anything to your son, check around to see if you can find a more student-friendly school. Look for the things I've mentioned in the last couple of chapters; *especially* look for small teacher loads and class size and flexible grouping—heterogeneous if possible, at least in English and social studies.

If you can find such a school and are pretty sure you can have your son admitted, talk to him about it. I had somewhat this same situation with my son. He wasn't that unhappy in his junior high, but the high school was pretty rigidly leveled, and the teachers had large student loads. Because I taught in Concord, he could attend the school there free of charge as a faculty child. And my school in Concord has low teacher-student ratios and very little leveling in English and social studies. So I talked to him about it. Of course, I knew it would be hard. He had been in his current district since second grade. We agreed finally that he would try it for one semester. At the end of the first semester, I promised him, he could return to his old school if he wanted to.

This is a technique a woman who suffers panic attacks taught me. In any difficult situation, you have a greater chance of sticking it out and even enjoying it if you have an escape. For this woman it means that if she has to attend a long dinner where her husband is a speaker, they take two cars. Then she can leave early if she starts to become uncomfortable. Just knowing she has an escape, she explained to me, often makes it possible for her to stay.

So that's how I set it up with my son, and it worked well. Concord was a much better school for him. For the first time in a number of years he was in classes with lots of good students, and after a while he realized that he was really a good student too. I think his whole image of himself in regard to school changed. Plus his reading and writing skills shot way up since he was in more challenging courses—but courses in which he could still be successful.

So you might try this with your child. If it's your daughter who is the reluctant reader, tell her you want her to try a new school for one semester. Explain why. Tell her again and again that you know she's bright and capable: you just want her to be in a school where she has a better chance to show it.

Of course, if she absolutely refuses, you're stuck. You have to leave her where she is, because with her mind set like that, she won't give the new school a fair shot anyway. But if she agrees, go ahead and make the change. You will have to keep your word if she wants to transfer back, but if the school is truly more student-friendly, she probably won't. For one thing, I believe a school that treats students well also encourages students to respect each other and to treat each other well. She may find not just the teachers, but also the students, more to her liking in the new school.

Which Class?

Let's assume you are doing your best with schools and watching the situation closely. Class choice is the next problem. If your school has leveling in the courses requiring reading, you are probably going to have to allow your son or daughter to be put into a lower level. There's a good chance that the books taught in the upper levels will just be too hard and (to her) boring. The bad thing about lower levels is that she'll be in with demoralized kids who think they're dumb and so don't want to work. Another bad thing is that she'll probably be given a lot of busywork to do: vocabulary exercises, grammar drill—stuff that won't help her at all. The good points are that the work will probably be easy enough that she can get all high grades if she wants to, and she'll have relatively little homework. That means she'll have more time at home to be reading the magazines and books you're getting her. Once kids start reading, reading levels go up pretty quickly. In just a year it may be possible to ask her if she's interested in moving to a higher level. If she is, suggest she talk to her teacher about it. If the teacher isn't agreeable—which may happen because teachers sometimes get kids typed in their minds—ask your daughter if she would like you to do a parental override. I think parents can do this in most states. If she's at the stage of reading books pretty regularly, she can probably do the work of a higher level.

But suppose your son, at this point, has *very* low reading skills and is having a lot of trouble passing the low-level courses. Or suppose he's in a school with mixed classes, and he just can't keep up. What do you do?

If he is reading a lot at home and isn't too demoralized at school, you might sit tight and wait for him to catch up. But if the situation is going downhill—if he is refusing to even try anymore—then you have to do something.

What If He's Failing?

First, of course, make sure the failure really is a reading failure. I mentioned in the last chapter that most massive failing in high school, I'm convinced, is caused by emotional problems. But some failure is caused by reading problems, and certainly a reading problem makes any emotional problem even more difficult. And *whatever* the cause, you have to do something.

First, of course, talk to your son. What does he want to do? He could switch to a lower-level course, if there is one. He could get tutoring. He could (probably, if he's failing) get special education assistance. He could perhaps switch to a more flexible teacher.

Let me explain the special education option here first.

Do You Want Special Education Services?

Although there is a federal law (Public Law 94–142) that requires schools to offer a certain level of special education services, some states have laws that mandate additional services. The federal law permits states to mandate that students fit into a certain category of disabilities. For example, in most states a student has to be diagnosed as learning disabled to receive special ed. help for a reading problem. In Massachusetts a student doesn't have to fit into a category, he just has to be "in need of special services." But if your child's reading is so poor that he is failing courses, you can probably ask for a core evaluation. And there's a good chance that he will be offered services after the evaluation. (If he isn't, you can go the legal route and demand services, but frankly I'm not sure if special education services, at least for a poor reader, are worth all that trouble.)

There are pros and cons about using special education services for poor readers. One con, as I mentioned before, is that in most states the kids have to be officially labeled— probably learning disabled, but maybe mentally retarded, or emotionally disabled. You really don't want your kid labeled like that, if you can help it. The other con is that the kind of help available for poor readers is usually resource room help at the student's school. Special ed. tutors or teachers basically try to tutor the student through his classes. Sometimes classes in individual English are offered, but usually only to students who are extremely low in reading skills. Of course, if your son is in this category, you might want to consider this option. My problem with the special ed. courses I've seen is that the kids seem to do relatively little reading in them. Reading is taught as a skill, with canned exercises and "special" reading material, and the kids are rarely given the kind of reading material (comics and magazines and individual books) that I've seen work.

But there are two good points to having your child brought under the special ed. law. One is that your child will get a lot more individual attention than he would otherwise. And some of the special ed. tutors and teachers are loving, supportive people. They can give your child the kind of help with his work that is sometimes hard for a child to accept from a parent.

The other plus to special ed. is that it gives you legal leverage with the school. Under the federal special ed. law the state must find a learning situation that is appropriate for your child. Under the law, if the public school is not appropriate, the school system is supposed to pay for a placement in a school that is—usually a special private school. Of course, most schools go to great lengths to resist such placements because they are so expensive. If there is a private special ed. school you want your son in, you may have to go to court to get your school system to pay.

I'd really hesitate before going this far. If your son (or daughter) is just a very poor reader, I don't think I'd have a lot of faith that a special ed. school could help him. What can they do? The track record of special ed. in general is not great for overcoming reading problems. Too often they use canned programs, exercises, everything that I'm convinced doesn't work.

Also, there is a real stigma attached to going to a "special" school. We have a special, in-school alternative program for kids who aren't passing mainstream classes in our school. The kids have dubbed it "the rubber room." There's even a stigma attached to going to a school resource room, even if only in your son's mind. But you can use this legal leverage another way (always, of course, with your son's agreement). You can vaguely threaten to sue for a private placement, and then say, well, maybe if your son were transferred into *this* course with *this* teacher things might work out. That way you can have your son placed in the classrooms of the warmest, most flexible teachers. Sometimes just doing that is enough to get your son working again.

But again, only do this with the full concurrence of your son. Remember, after the age of eight or nine, you're letting him call the shots. Believe me, there's no other way to go.

There's one other aspect of special ed. I should mention.

It has recently become common in my school district, which is rather affluent, for parents to hire special education advocates to attend school meetings with them. The idea, I guess, is that the advocate is an expert on the law and will ensure the school's compliance.

I have reservations about this practice, except in the case of severely handicapped youngsters. Severely handicapped youngsters require very expensive placements, and you may well need to bring in an advocate to ensure your child receives the kind of educational services he needs.

But sometimes bringing in an advocate for a student with only mild disabilities actually hurts the student. Advocates will push for a lot of restrictive language in the child's education plan. I've seen plans that prohibit teachers from taking points off for misspelled words. This always seemed to me like putting a kid in a basketball game and declaring to the referee that all balls that even touch the rim are to be counted as baskets, because your child has poor eye-hand coordination. You're just not preparing your son to live in the real world.

Instead, help him proofread for spelling errors at home, or get him a good computer with a spell-checker, and tell him to do the best job he can on in-class writing. Let your son and the teacher figure out how to deal with his spelling problem in class. It's your *son's* problem. Don't run interference for him, especially with an advocate as a hired gun. Remember, you want your child to grow up to be joyous and self-confident. That won't happen if you fight his battles for him.

And I guess this leads to my real problem with massive special ed. resource room help. By late elementary school, and certainly by junior high and high school, the ideal is for a kid to find the help he needs himself. If he's having trouble in English, it's best if he approach his English teacher and ask for extra help. For one thing, the English teacher knows exactly what her assignment is and will be better able to help him. For another thing, getting help from an English teacher doesn't mark him out as "dumb," as going to the resource room can. And it's help he has to initiate. Kids are usually assigned to the resource room and get help whether they want it or not. This results in more work being done over the short term, but not, I think, over the long term—because the student's self-esteem is eroded.

So if your daughter or son simply cannot make it through mainstream classes without special ed. help, sure—agree to the help. If your son really needs the help but doesn't want it, try the escape deal. See if he'll try the help for one semester, and if he doesn't find it useful he can stop going. But if he is getting special ed. help you should always be striving to help him move out of it as soon as possible. Independence is the goal!

So now your son is in an adequate school, he may be getting resource room help, he's in the best classes he can manage, but he's still having many day-to-day problems. What do you do?

Day-to-Day Problems

I think most day-to-day problems center on reading assignments that your son is not quite up to yet. He'll be given a handout in social studies, or a lab description in biology, or a book in English that he really can't quite make sense of.

First, of course, you do active listening, and let him express his frustration. Agree that the material is boring (often a poor reader's word for "hard"). Ask him if he's comfortable with talking to the teacher about his difficulty with this reading. If he is, great. Just hope the teacher is sympathetic.

If he won't talk to the teacher, ask him if he'd like you to help. Say you're willing to read the material over and summarize it for him. Would he like you to do that? If he's agreeable, do that for him. After all, you have him reading at home, right? You're working him up through magazines and comics and easy books. Sooner or later he'll be able to handle this material himself. And I really think listening to a summary from you—to keep him from failing in school—and then going off to page through his latest edition of *Soccer World* is much more beneficial for him.

You may find that your son gets in place some survival strategies himself. And that's fine. He may get a friend to help him; he may skim the material and get enough out of it to get by; he may go out and buy Cliffs Notes. Of course, I have the instinctive revulsion at Cliffs Notes that all English teachers have—but I think as long as we assign kids books that are simply too hard for them, we can't complain about Cliffs Notes. Certainly, as a parent I don't think you should complain. If it really bothers you, pretend you don't see the notorious little yellow and black pamphlet.

Writing Assignments

If your son is a very poor reader, there is a 100 percent chance that he is also a poor writer. Keep in mind that he can't *help* being a poor writer now, any more than a two-year-old can help saying "Go bed, no!" He hasn't had enough written language input to become a good writer.

In some ways, it's easier to be the parent of a poor writer than the teacher. The parent doesn't have to look at an essay or story that a newly turned on, enthusiastic student has spent hours on and is very proud of—and give it a B minus or a C (because it really isn't terrific, and you do have to maintain some kind of grading standards). You, the parent, can just smile enthusiastically and say, "Oh, I love this story! Your main character is so funny, and I love the descriptions of the castle." Then you can tactfully ask if he'd like some help in proofreading. (When you help a poor reader proofread, just *tell* him the correct spelling and punctuation. If you draw it out and make him guess, he'll stop asking you.) But be enthusiastic about whatever he shows you. That's the job of the parent. Always be encouraging.

I wouldn't make many suggestions for change, other than proofreading suggestions. Confidence is everything in writing—as in much else—and the last thing you want to do is to nitpick at his work. Hopefully his teacher won't nitpick either, but even if she does at least you're encouraging him.

Of course, only help your child with his writing if he wants you to. Some parents don't understand that kids need to initiate the request for help. I had a student in class one time who wasn't doing much writing. This was surprising, because the kids were writing mysteries, and there was great enthusiasm for this assignment among most of my students. I was being barraged with endless stories of stabbings and shootings and strangulations—kids were stopping me in the hall to show me stories. But she wasn't writing much. Then she casually remarked one day that she was going to be grounded for the next week.

"Why?" I heard her friend ask.

"Because I didn't show my mother my history report before I turned it in, and she said that if I got less than a B on it I'd be grounded."

I was horrified but managed to keep my editorial comments to myself. But I understood her less-than-enthusiastic approach to writing.

So even though you know that the paper your son is going to turn in is terrible, don't help him at all unless he asks you to. His writing will improve, with practice, and with the reading he is doing. But it will never improve if he stops trying—and the fastest way to ensure he stops trying is for you to be too intrusive about helping him.

But what if he hands in a terribly written paper? Almost no teacher will fail a high school student who is really trying—unless, of course, you've gone against my recommendation and placed your child in a high-level class that he can't handle. If you've done this, the teacher may be feeling a little hostile, since it's very difficult to deal with a poor reader and poor writer in a homogeneously grouped high-level class. Then she really may fail him. And you'll have to move him to a lower-level class anyway.

So while you may gently help your son with his papers, you can only do it when he asks, and you can only give him the kind of help he asks for. You can't write the paper for him. There's no future in it. His writing won't improve if you're doing most of it. And he'll never survive in college.

If you can afford it, however, there is one important way you can help your child with writing. Get him a computer. For some reason many poor readers, especially boys, also have poor handwriting, and writing is slow and laborious for them. Plus, of course, their spelling is terrible. A good computer, with a good spell-checker, can make a poor writer more independent. It also does wonders for his self-confidence to see his work all neatly typed up. Important to this project is that you somehow get him to take a typing or keyboarding course, so his typing isn't forever slow and laborious. You might be able to find a good software course that teaches typing. You won't need to sign him up for a word processing course. Modern kids are born with the computer gene; he'll figure out how to move text around while you're still working on how to turn the damn thing on. But do try to encourage, bribe, threaten, or cajole him into that typing course. If he can work comfortably on the computer, you'll find a huge, immediate gain in his writing fluency. His actual written language—the structure and complexity of his sentences—won't improve much until he is reading more. But the computer can be a big help in keeping him viable in school—and in helping him actually enjoy writing.

Long-Term Outlook

For twenty years, now, I've seen kids with very poor read-ing skills come into my classroom. Since I'm a high school teacher, by the time I get these kids they've experienced years of failure, of feeling dumb, of not being able to keep up. What does this experience do to them?

Often—not always, but often—there's a special sweet-ness to kids who have had to struggle extra hard. I don't think it's any coincidence that, when I think back to my favorite students over the years, a huge number of them were kids with serious reading problems. They are often very kind, accepting people, and always very grateful for any help I could give them.

You may say this isn't much comfort for you now. Your problem is to get your son through U.S. history, with a teacher who continually assigns reading that he can't do. I don't want to minimize your unhappiness over this, but it might comfort you to know that this really searing experi-ence for your child—of day after day attending classes and being assigned work that is just too hard for him—may give him reserves of compassion and strength that will enable him to pull through life experiences that would completely sink another person.

I guess my last bit of advice is to tell you to relax, as much as possible, about his school performance. In the long run—and you're always thinking of that, right?— good grades in school don't mean all that much. Face it: if your son or daughter is coming very late to reading, he or she is not going to get into a prestigious, competitive college. And that's okay. There are plenty of very good colleges around that take kids with low high school grades. If necessary, your child can start at a local junior college—or not even go to college (although I wouldn't advise that). But the point is that you want your child to be a competent, independent adult who loves reading. So you can't be too intrusive and crazy about any high school failure he's having. If you have him reading at home, the failure is temporary.

Relax! Trust your kid!

A Final Note

As I was finishing the manuscript of this book, I was given a copy of *The Power of Reading: Insights from the Research,* by Stephen Krashen (Libraries Unlimited, Inc., Englewood, Colorado, 1993). Without much enthusiasm, I sat down to read what I thought would be simply another book telling me that I needed to teach comprehension skills and vocabulary to my students.

When I finished reading the book my hands were shaking. Using an extensive search of available research as his authority—much of it small studies done years ago, and much of it very current research (he cites over 200 references)—Krashen advises teachers to teach literacy by encouraging what he calls "free voluntary reading." Specifically he says that "reading is the only way, the only way that we become good readers, develop a good writing style, an adequate vocabulary, advanced grammar, and the only way we become good spellers." He supports comic books and teenage romances as "conduits" to more complex literature. The following are some of his conclusions:

- The case against direct reading instruction is overwhelming.
- Direct language instruction with drills and exercises is merely testing.
- Teaching vocabulary lists is inefficient—the time is better spent reading alone.
- Well-read people write well because they have subconsciously acquired good writing style.

- Creating a print-rich environment is a key.
- Television is not the culprit in the "literacy crisis."

To see the conclusions that I've come to, after twenty years in a classroom, finally reinforced by a researcher is simply overwhelming to me.

And so I end this book on a much more hopeful note than I began it. Maybe our schools can be changed. Maybe, with the backing of the research that Krashen cites, our classrooms will become places of joyous reading and booksharing. Maybe all of the vocabulary exercises and "teaching" of comprehension skills will finally cease.

Imagine a country where all the people loved books. Our social, economic, and political fabric would be completely altered. It's impossible to imagine all of the changes, but it's a country I'd love to live in.

And maybe, if we all keep plugging away, it's a country we *can* live in. For the first time, I feel a little hope.

A List of Reading Suggestions

I THINK FEW PARENTS HAVE DIFFICULTY FINDING PIC-
ture books for their small children. Little kids love being
read to, there is a wonderful supply of vivid, exciting books
available, and small children haven't yet been taught in
school that reading is work, and therefore unpleasant. Picture books your young child will like are fun and easy to
find. Any library or bookstore will be full of them. Dr. Seuss
books and the Berenstain Bears books are the two groups
of picture books most fondly remembered by my students.

This list is concentrated on books for children from the
age of eight or nine up through high school age. Every author on this list has been recommended to me by my students, my own children, nieces and nephews, or other
young friends. The comments in quotation marks are direct
quotes from them.

After the main list, I've added an addendum titled Classic
Books. These are books not included in my main list, but
are often recommended or assigned by teachers. The purpose of this addendum is twofold: it should help you recognize the best books from your child's summer reading
lists, and, in some cases, will suggest ways of helping your
child with an assigned book.

Although all of the books on the main list have been recommended by young people, not all kids will like all of these books. If there is one thing I've learned after raising three children and teaching for twenty years, it's that all kids are different. A book one child loves will be hated by another one. However, once you know the *kind* of books your child likes—mysteries, fantasies, whatever—you can see in this list which authors in that category are most popular with other kids. If your son likes fantasy, then there is a good chance he will enjoy most of the books on the fantasy list—but don't be surprised if he thinks most books on the mystery list are dry and boring.

Some kids, of course, happily read many different kinds of books. But these are usually kids well on their way to being competent, sophisticated readers. If your son is only starting to read, don't be surprised if he reads only suspense. Don't be surprised if your daughter reads only growing-up books.

Accordingly, I have organized the lists by authors' names within several categories. I've listed the authors who write juvenile books at the beginning of each category, since juvenile books are always shelved separately from adult ones. To find a Roald Dahl title, you have to go to the children's section of your bookstore or library.

It's important to realize that just because a book is listed as a "juvenile" doesn't mean that it's an easy, simple-minded book. The term "juvenile" simply refers to the intended age group. Some juvenile books are further designated "Young Adult," and are usually shelved in a special corner of the children's section. So the "juvenile" designation covers a large age range. And some books, like *A Separate Peace* by John Knowles, might be shelved in either the adult or children's section. If you have trouble finding a certain book, of course, just ask the librarian or book seller.

Some avid readers start crossing over to adult titles as early as fourth or fifth grade. Poorer readers cross later. Almost all of my readers seem to go back and forth for awhile. Currently, one of my excellent American Lit. students is reading the Anne of Green Gables books. You want your kids to *read*. Don't worry about the supposed age range of the books.

What about books that have a movie version available? A number of the books I list (almost *all* of Stephen King's books, for example) have a video version out now. Should you rent it first to arouse interest in the novel?

On the whole, I like kids to see the video *after* they've finished the book, because then they are almost always horrified at how much has been cut. I don't point out to them that you have to cut a book to make a good movie; I just point out smugly (and falsely) that books are *always* better than movies. Kids who see the movie first may be anxious to start that book, but often have trouble finishing it, because they know what's going to happen. When you read slowly and with difficulty, wondering *what's going to happen next* is usually what gets you through a book. Very good readers, on the other hand, often *will* read a book after they've enjoyed the movie, because they want to find out more detail about the story. So rent a movie first for good readers, but not for poor or average readers.

One thing you may notice on this list is that, for some of the most popular authors like Stephen King, Danielle Steel, and Robert Parker, I don't have comments from kids on the most recent titles. This is usually just a matter of student access. Very recent titles are still in hardback—out of budget range—and semi-recent titles are still hard to get at libraries, and impossible to find at flea markets. So most of my students, who are not yet at the "I'll spend some of my money on new books" stage, read the less recent titles that are easily available in my classroom or in the school library. I have listed some of the newer titles for you, since you may have an easier time finding them than you will finding some of the older titles in bookstores.

And another aspect to this list: these are just the books that *my* students, children, and acquaintances in this little town of Concord, Massachusetts happen to love. I know that there are many, many other wonderful books for young people that I don't list. I think the value of this list lies in showing you what kind of books kids read—and showing you that kids really can *love* books. If nothing on this list seems right for your child or teenager, you should ask a local librarian or bookseller to make suggestions, since they should know what is popular in your section of the country.

Entries that I've marked with an asterisk (*) indicate authors that are almost sure winners with kids.

One other thing: When you find other wonderful books, I would love to hear about them. You can write to me c/o Crown Publishers, 201 East 50th St., New York, NY 10022.

Because I recommend comics and magazines as an easy entry into reading, I'll start with them.

COMIC BOOKS

There are two main kinds of comics: those that are usually printed as cartoon strips in a newspaper first and then published in book form and sold in bookstores, and those that are really weekly or monthly magazines and sold in newsstands or special comic book stores. Books of cartoons are usually shelved by author in the Humor section of a bookstore. Newsstand and comics stores shelve their comics by title, since a variety of authors will write for the same titles.

CARTOON BOOKS FOUND IN REGULAR BOOKSTORES
Davis, Jim. Garfield comics. These are very easy reading, but many kids, boys especially, seem to read them throughout elementary and junior high. "I read far too much Garfield for my sanity," one of my very sane high school students remarked, and from a thirteen-year-old friend: "Just a funny kind of book."

Hergé. Tintin books. This is a comic series about a young reporter who solves mysteries and has adventures all over the world. Very popular with my students when they were younger. Some of the titles are available in the original French.

Larson, Gary. *The Far Side.* Very popular with my students. These comics make me feel old because I can't see any sense in them at all. The kids have to *explain* them to me. "Very bizarre ... Everyone's a dork. Sort of a parody on life."

Trudeau, G. B. Doonesbury comics. These comics are especially popular with students who have some interest in history or the political scene, although I've also seen kids who can hardly read pore over them. They are very satiric and funny.

***Watterson, Bill.** Calvin and Hobbes comics. Very easy reading and incredibly popular with almost all of my students. I had a bulletin board of *Calvin and Hobbes* strips one year and could hardly get my students to their seats. A good friend of mine describes how her thirteen-year-old son follows her around the house when she's trying to work, reading *Calvin and Hobbes* comic strips to her. His comment: "It's fun to read because it's about an average six-year-old boy and his big imagination on viewing the world." From one of my high school kids: "Kid and his stuffed animal. Kind of hallucinogenic. My favorite. They make situations that wouldn't be funny, funny."

REGULAR COMICS FOUND IN NEWSSTANDS AND COMIC BOOK STORES

Note: The world of comics is fast changing and slightly bewildering to an adult like me who doesn't keep up with it. Many thanks to Bob Gerrity, of a small comics store in Maynard, Massachusetts called Comically Speaking. He spent much time talking to me and introducing me to many of his comic-reading customers. Comics seem to fall into two main groups: funny comics aimed at a younger audience, and adventure comics aimed at kids, usually boys, around ten and up.

Funny Comics. Published mostly by Disney and Harvey House, these comics are very easy reading, and an excellent way to help young children become independent readers. Some favorites: *Archie* ("A teenage soap opera"), *Richie Rich* ("Life-styles of the rich and famous"), *Casper*, *Little Dot*, *Jetsons*, *Yogi Bear*, *Woody Woodpecker*.

Adventure Comics. The two main publishers here are Marvel and D.C. The style and vocabulary of these comics are more sophisticated. They're popular with later elementary, junior high, and high school readers. The most popular group of titles seems to be the X-Men and Punisher series. The Punisher comics are the most violent. Other favorites: *Amazing Spiderman*, *The Avengers*, *Batman*, *Cyberforce* ("Great art, not much plot"), *Elfquest* (also published in bound books found in bookstores or hobby stores), and *Ghost Rider*.

MAGAZINES

Many bookstores now have a huge selection of magazines. I think it would be worth your while to spend some time at one, looking for titles to interest your child. You also might try hobby shops and specialty stores. Model train magazines, for example, would be found in hobby shops. Tower Records (or any large CD and tape store, probably) has a truly amazing selection of music magazines, and if you have a son whose whole goal in life is to have his own rock band, this would be the place to start.

What follow are the magazines that my students love or

remember loving as kids. There are many, many other wonderful magazines available.

FOR YOUNGER, PRE–HIGH SCHOOL READERS

American Girl. This magazine is published by the Pleasant Company as a companion to its selection of very popular dolls. The magazine "has dolls from different time periods. Has pictures of dolls and what it was like back then. People write in and tell about themselves. Has a paper doll every month and clothes for the paper doll. So cute. All the stuff you can get for their dolls." My younger daughter and all of her friends loved this magazine.

Boy's Life. The magazine of the Boy Scouts of America. Articles on sports, crafts, the outdoors. "Covers a lot of things." Good for kids who like the outdoors.

Cracked. A satiric magazine, much like *Mad.* Especially good for that adamant nonreading twelve-year-old boy.

Discover. "Always has the latest updates in science." This is a good magazine even for adults. It makes science understandable.

Disney Adventure Magazine. "Full of pictures, short stories, and comics. Has games and puzzles in the back."

Highlights. "I loved it when I was little. Puzzles, games, short stories, riddles and jokes." A lot of students remembered loving this magazine.

In Your Backyard. "Fun, wildlife for kids. Great pictures."

*Mad Magazine. "Comedy. Makes fun of everything. I loved *Mad.*" This magazine is the first thing you should try with a nonreading boy of ten or so. It's even better than *Cracked.*

Ranger Rick. "I loved the cute fuzzy animals." Another outdoor magazine.

*Sports Illustrated for Kids. "Easy reading and good posters and punchouts." A must try for young athletes. A magazine that can be read on the run to all of those endless games.

3-2-1-Contact. "Science for kids." This was another magazine mentioned again and again.

Zillions: Consumer Reports for Kids. "Makes you feel old! Has annual toy tests. Tests the most popular toys." I was surprised how many students mentioned enjoying this magazine.

Magazines for Older Readers
Bass Player. "The *best* magazine for anyone who plays bass." One of my students insisted I include this very specialized title, which shows you how attached kids can get to special interest magazines.

Consumer Reports. This title came up again and again when I asked what magazines my students liked. Surprised me!

Cosmopolitan. "Like *Glamour* but more articles. Has all the new fashions. Interesting articles."

Dolls. "Shows different dolls you can get, and sometimes tells you how to make dolls. It has a doll gallery and stuff about old fashioned dolls." I think this is a magazine for collectors as well as children.

Ebony. "Magazine telling about all kinds of topics nationwide and worldwide. Geared to African-American audience."

Essence. Another magazine for an African-American audience. A number of my students reported enjoying it.

Glamour. "It's good. Fashions. Do's and don't's. Horoscopes." A lot of teenage girls mentioned this one too.

International Wildlife. "True stories. A lot of pictures."

Jet. "Black magazine. News. Geared towards adults but I started reading it at eight or nine."

Mademoiselle. Another fashion magazine teenage girls enjoy.

Modern Drummer. For the band member.

Motor Trend. For the car-crazy adolescent.

National Geographic. I wonder how many generations of kids have collected these? "EXCELLENT. AN 'A'."

Newsweek. "Has interesting articles, and little quotes by people in the spotlight."

Popular Mechanics. "Good magazine. A-plus."

Popular Science. "Very informative. A-plus."

Practical Horseman. "About both riding and taking care of horses, but mostly about riding. All English, no Western."

Reader's Digest. This title came up occasionally. I think it's a good magazine to leave around the house. Kids pick it up and read short pieces.

Road and Track. Another good one for the car-crazy teenager.

Rolling Stone. Very popular with teenagers. I used to take my son's old copies to school when I had to monitor in-school suspension. I could keep a whole room quiet with *Rolling Stone* and *Sports Illustrated.*

Sassy. "Teen related stories so it is fun to read." A number of girls mentioned loving this one.

Seventeen. "I love looking at the models, the facials, the nails. Your Ten Hair Problems. Before and After. I like the tests: how you should have your room, what kind of perfume." A very popular magazine with teenagers. They seem to read this when they're too busy to read anything else.

Ski Magazine. "Good guide to premier ski areas. Started reading at age eight."

Sports Illustrated. Incredibly popular with teenagers who love sports. My older daughter tells me that when her copy used to arrive at her dorm, she had lines of people wanting to read it as soon as she was finished. It's expensive, because it comes every week, but it will keep your athlete reading.

Teen. "Same thing as *Seventeen* but *Teen* is designed for a younger crowd, eleven, twelve, thirteen. Always has these questions about your period. Has Ask Your Doctor, Ask Jack and Ask Jill. You can write in any kind of question you want. Has Dear Beauty Editor and sometimes has cartoons."

Teen Beat. Another popular teenage magazine. Focuses on stars.

Time. "Good for research and stuff."

YM (Young & Modern) "Like *Teen* but better. It's awesome. Has articles and stories about topics—suicide, drugs, real-life topics." Almost every teenage girl I asked about magazines mentioned this one.

GROWING UP AND COMING-OF-AGE BOOKS

I think this category has the highest proportion of books that kids really fall in love with. Many of these books speak right to their own fears and hopes.

JUVENILE AUTHORS

Babbitt, Natalie. *Tuck Everlasting.* This tells the story of a ten-year-old girl who finds a family that drinks from a spring with water that keeps the family from aging. A book many of my students remember reading in elementary school.

*Blume, Judy. Blume has many titles, all very popular. Most of her books are for elementary school children, such as: *Tales of a Fourth Grade Nothing; Are You There, God? It's Me, Margaret; It's Not the End of the World; Tiger Eyes; Deenie; Freckle Juice; Blubber; Otherwise Known as Sheila the Great.* "I read all her books. My favorite author in the third and fourth grade." A special favorite: *Superfudge* "is funny. Tells how annoying a brother can be and how you can be so frustrated with him. Really good book. Parents should read—would learn the point of view of a kid." My students caution me about *Forever:* "Two seniors in high school fall in love. Relationship is graphic. Don't give to kids until at least junior high." But for a number of my nonreading sophomore girls, *Forever* is the first book I've seen them finish. "An excellent book. Katherine loved Michael very much, but knew her attraction and longingness to spend time with another couldn't be denied. She learned her mother was right."

*Cleary, Beverly. Many, many of my students loved her books in elementary school. Her Henry Huggins books are probably the easiest to read, but it's the Ramona series that is remembered most fondly by my students. One special favorite: *Ramona Quimby, Age Eight:* "Showed a really good point of view of the young child, when you have a teenage sibling and the parents always take their side." Another student said simply: "I loved every single Ramona book." Another favorite is the trilogy about Ralph the Mouse: *The Mouse and the Motorcycle, Runaway Ralph,* and *Ralph S. Mouse.*

Coombs, Patricia. Dorrie the Little Witch series books. Some titles: *Dorrie and the Blue Witch, Dorrie and the Birthday Eggs.* These are wonderful books for seven- or eight-year-old girls who are just starting to read chapter books. They're short, have pictures, and show a little witch who always gets in trouble, but ends up as a brave heroine who solves mysteries. Both my daughters loved these books; we combed bookstores and libraries looking for yet another one.

*Dahl, Roald. Dahl was by far the most popular author mentioned by mid-elementary school readers. Along with Stan and Janice Berenstain (of Berenstain Bears fame), he was the most loved children's author. Almost every student remembered loving his books. *James and the Giant Peach* "showed children can be independent and anything can happen." About the book titled *The BFG:* "The best, best, best, funniest book." A high school student: "I read *Charlie and the Chocolate Factory* four times a year, usually all in one night." *The Twits:* "They were dirty and Mr. Twit had crumbs in his beard so when he's hungry he can reach his tongue out and get a snack!"

Danziger, Paula. She's written many teenage novels about growing up problems. Popular with girls in late elementary and junior high school. Comic tone, easy reading. Some titles: *Can You Sue Your Parents for Malpractice? The Cat Ate My Gym Suit, There's a Bat in Bunk Five.*

Farley, Walter. The Black Stallion series, including *The Black Stallion Returns, The Black Stallion and Flame.* The Farley books were mentioned to me again and again by kids who liked riding horses. They are popular with elementary through junior high age kids. There are many different titles. "Awesome. Really good."

Gilbreth, Frank B., and Ernestine G. Carey. *Cheaper by the Dozen.* This old children's classic doesn't seem to lose its popularity. A few of my American Literature students read it every year, and report really enjoying it. I wouldn't give it to an elementary school student who's not an excellent reader. Save it for junior high and high school students.

Guy, Rosa. *The Friends, Edith Jackson, Ruby.* Guy writes about the tribulations of a girl from Trinidad who comes to New York. Popular with my African-American high school students. Another title: *Paris, Pee Wee and Big Dog.* "Cute story."

Henry, Marguerite. *Misty of Chincoteague.* These books are a must for the horse lover. I first heard of these books about fifteen years ago in Norfolk, when one of my best readers wrote that they were her all-time favorite books; she read them again and again. Sequels: *Sea Star: Orphan of Chincoteague* and *Stormy: Misty's Foal.*

*Hinton, S. E. Young Adult author. Susie Hinton wrote *The Outsiders* when she was seventeen, and it's as close as you'll come to an infallible book for a poor-reading teenage boy or girl. Even good readers like her books. Some kids read them again and again. *The Outsiders:* "I can relate to some of the experiences in it, the fact that people judge others by the way they look or by the people they hang around with. My favorite book ever." Other Hinton titles: *That Was Then, This Is Now:* "Liked it because it's about kids and the dumb things kids do." "I don't want it to end," said another reader. Also popular is *Rumble Fish*: "About people my own age I can relate to. Good fights in it."

Hope, Laura L. The Bobbsey Twins series. Sample titles: *The Bobbsey Twins' Adventure in the Country, The Bobbsey Twins' Adventures with Baby May.* About a family with two sets of twins. These are very simple books, suitable for elementary school students, that I thought were dated. A number of my students, however, remember loving them. "I've always liked the twins thing. I have the whole collection."

Klein, Norma. Klein writes many short, quick books for junior high and high school students. Some titles: *Give Me One Good Reason; It's Not What You'd Expect; It's Okay If You Don't Love Me; Sunshine; Taking Sides.* One of my students especially liked *Angel Face:* "About a guy named Jason whose parents are getting divorced. It was real life-like." *Love Is One of the Choices:* "I really love this book. I really like how Norma Klein writes. It's very realistic."

Lewis, Linda. She has written many titles, including *Is There Life after Boys? My Heart Belongs to That Boy, We Hate Everything but Boys, We Love only Older Boys.* Her name was given to me by an eighth grader who said she usually didn't like to read, but she loved Lewis's books. "Starts when the girl is twelve and shows the problems as she gets older. I could read one in a day."

Lowry, Lois. Anastasia books. Sample titles: *Anastasia Again!, Anastasia, Ask Your Analyst.* These are humorous accounts of Anastasia Krupnik dealing with common growing-up problems, such as moving, doing school reports, and working for a neighbor. Many students remembered reading these books in elementary school. "I used to love them.

My mother bought them all. About a girl in school, and her life. Wicked good."

MacDonald, Betty. Mrs. Piggle-Wiggle books. These are wonderful books for elementary school children. They swept my daughter's fifth-grade class. Sample titles: *Mrs. Piggle-Wiggle, Mrs. Piggle-Wiggle's Magic.* About a funny lady who helps kids. Mrs. Penzil's children wouldn't eat a good diet. "Potter only ate peanut butter and poppy seeds. Pamela ate weenies and bananas, and Percy ate cookies, candy, marshmallows, cake, ice cream and root beer. And Mrs. Piggle-Wiggle lives in an upside-down house."

*Martin, Ann. The Baby-Sitters Club books. This extensive series, all written personally by Ann Martin, details the growing-up experiences of a group of girls who form a club to provide companionship and babysitting services. Many, many of my kids reported loving these in elementary school. "I really liked them, and I could read one a night if I stayed up late." There's a spinoff series now called The Baby-Sitters Club Mysteries, as well as a series for beginning readers called The Baby-Sitters Little Sister.

Naylor, Phyllis R. Her series of Alice books are very popular with late elementary or early junior high students. Some titles: *Alice in Rapture, Sort of; The Agony of Alice; Reluctantly Alice.* "About a girl named Alice McKinley, and the funny things that happen to her. Her mother died so she just has a father and an older brother." Naylor also writes a wide variety of other books. A favorite is *Walking Through the Dark.* "Takes place in the 1940s. Family was in Germany. Nazis pushed them out because they were Jewish."

O'Brien, Robert. *Mrs. Frisby and the Rats of NIMH.* "It's the kind of story you want to believe, that rats could have tunnels underground, because they were planning on building a nation under ground. They had everything, gardens, electricity . . . " The sequel is *Rasco and the Rats of NIMH* by the author's daughter, Jane Conly.

O'Dell, Scott. *Island of the Blue Dolphins.* This is the story of an Indian girl who lives alone on an island off the coast of California. It's set in the early nineteenth century. I'd give it to late elementary and junior high students. "It made me cry. Great." Other titles: *Zia* (the sequel to *Island*), *The Black Pearl, Child of Fire,* and *Sing Down the Moon.*

*Pascal, Francine. Sweet Valley High series for junior high–aged girls, Sweet Valley Twins series for late elementary–aged girls, and Sweet Valley Kids for beginning readers. These books detail the growing-up trials of a pair of identical twins who are very dissimilar in their personalities. My own younger daughter loved the Twins series. We haunted bookstores, waiting for the next one to come out. "Showed a lot about how popularity works. How persuasive people can be. What kids do to losers, fat kids. Shows a lot of things that go on." A sophomore commented: "When I was seven years old there was nothing I wanted more than to be in high school. I think I read every Sweet Valley Twins book ever written in preparation for my teen life." One of my very best British Literature students wrote about the Sweet Valley High series: "Loved them, still read them when I'm bored."

Paterson, Katherine. Her *Bridge to Terabithia* is a "sad book but a good way to learn about death and that girls and boys can be friends together. Says death can happen to anyone." This is another book that came up again and again when I asked my students what books they loved as elementary school students Others of her books mentioned by my students include *The Great Gilly Hopkins* and *Jacob Have I Loved.*

Peck, Richard. Peck writes Young Adult titles that junior high and some younger high school students enjoy. *Don't Look and It Won't Hurt:* "About a girl who has an older sister who's a slut and a weird younger sister. Father ran out. Mother is messed up. In general, a messed-up family." Peck's *Father Figure* is also popular. It's about a boy who acts like a father to his younger brother, until they go for a visit with their real father. Peck writes mysteries too: *Through a Brief Darkness* and *Are You in the House Alone?* are also fairly popular.

Rawls, Wilson. *Where the Red Fern Grows.* A classic children's book that kids really do love. It's about a boy who saves up to buy two hunting dogs. "It was really sad and I couldn't stop reading it. I read it last April vacation, all vacation."

Rockwell, Thomas. *How to Eat Fried Worms.* A boy eats worms for a bet. Of course it's disgusting, but kids love it. Good for elementary school boys. "I thought it was great. I read it three times."

Selden, George. This is another author a lot of my students fondly remember from their elementary school days. Among his books are *Chester Cricket's New Home, Tucker's Countryside,* and the favorite: *The Cricket in Times Square.* "A little unrealistic with a mouse and cat talking, but it was enjoyable to read. Shows what it's like to live in inner-city New York, but kids can understand because it's told by a mouse and a cat and a cricket. Shows what it's like to be homeless."

Silverstein, Shel. *The Giving Tree* is essentially a fable "about a boy who took this tree and the tree gave him everything that he asked for. I always have liked it." Silverstein has also written a couple of books of poetry that kids love:

Where the Sidewalk Ends and *A Light in the Attic*. Many of my students were introduced to them in elementary school, but still love them in high school.

Smith, Betty. Junior high or high school girls seem to enjoy her books the most. *A Tree Grows in Brooklyn* is her best-known book. "About life in Brooklyn, New York, in the early nineteen hundreds. I like the way they tell the story. You feel like you're in the life of the person." *Joy in the Morning* has been very popular with some of my high school students. It's also set in the early nineteen hundreds, and is the story of a young married couple and the husband's struggle to finish college. *Maggie Now* is Smith's other book that students report loving.

Taylor, Mildred. *Roll of Thunder, Hear My Cry.* This is about life for a black family during the early part of the century in the South. Fairly good readers loved it; mediocre readers found it boring. Although it's often taught in junior high, I think high school students do better with it. The sequel is *Let the Circle Be Unbroken*.

Twain, Mark. Start with *Tom Sawyer*, which is a funny story of boys growing up in the nineteenth century. It's not difficult thematically, but the dialect takes time for some students to master. *The Adventures of Huckleberry Finn* is Twain's masterpiece, and kids seem to do best with this book if they're not given it too early, and if they're fairly good readers. I would wait until tenth or eleventh grade. Then they see the satire and the poignancy, and really enjoy it. "It reminds me of my childhood," a student remarked to me. Tell your teenagers that, after over a hundred years in print, *Huck Finn* is still one of the most censored books in school curriculums, and they'll be eager to read it. *A Connecticut Yankee in King Arthur's Court* is sometimes enjoyed by excellent readers who fell in love with Twain through *Huck Finn*, as is *The Prince and the Pauper*.

White, E. B. *Charlotte's Web* is a book virtually all my students remember loving in elementary school. "Motivates children not to be afraid of spiders. Tells about how farmers kill pigs and about farm life." *Stuart Little* was another favorite: "Small car theme. Model boats. Matchbox furniture. Smallness. Cuteness. Adventure." Another student described it more simply: "It's about a mouse who goes sailing. It's really cool."

Wilkinson, Brenda. *Ludell, Ludell and Willie, Ludell's New York Time.* I read these books after a number of my African-American students had fallen in love with them. They're about a Southern black girl who comes to New York to live. I found them poignant and moving, and especially successful with young black women. I wish Wilkinson would add to the series.

Wyss, Johann D. *The Swiss Family Robinson.* A classic adventure story. I'd give it to good readers in elementary school, and average readers in junior high or high school. A number of my students have fond memories of it.

ADULT GROWING-UP AND COMING-OF-AGE AUTHORS (Occasionally some of these authors will be shelved with young adult or juvenile books.)

*Andrews, V. C. Her books, which are usually about girls caught in horrible family situations, are almost infallible for junior high and high school girls (and some boys). She is incredibly popular with my students. "The books really get a hold of you and you have to finish them." She has different series, and the books really need to be read in order in each series. Start with *Flowers in the Attic.* It's really a book about child abuse. Children are locked in an attic for years so their mother can inherit money. "You learn how much people hate something they don't know anything about." After that series you might try the series that starts with *Dawn:* "a really loving family that's really poor and everyone hates the kids because they're very poor. Then Dawn finds out she was abducted from an uncaring rich family and has to go live with them." Or the one starting with *Heaven*. One of my former nonreaders wrote in one of her reports on the Heaven series: "I am excited to go to bed tonight so I can read!" *My Sweet Audrina*, not part of a series, is the favorite book of a number of her (many, many) fans. "Interesting because it showed that sometimes parents can really blow things out of proportion and screw things up."

Conroy, Pat. His books seem sophisticated to me, but many of my high school kids who aren't wonderful readers love him. His first person narratives make his books more accessible, but thematically I think he's too sophisticated for junior high kids. Wait for high school. *The Great Santini:* "About Bull Meecham and his family. Bull is a Marine pilot and he is really strict. Ben, his son, is the main character and is pretty tough. An awesome book." *The Prince of Tides*, the story of a young man trying to help come to terms with a very dysfunctional family background, always sweeps my American Literature classes. "I absolutely loved this book. I wished it could've gone on forever. Dealt with the whole 'New York, Psychiatric Era.' " *The Lords of Discipline* is another favorite, about the Citadel in South Carolina. I think it's the funniest of his books.

Dart, Iris R. *Beaches.* "About two young girls and how they become best friends." This book seems an exception to the general rule that average or poor readers don't finish reading books if they've seen the movie. A number of my high school girls have enjoyed this book. The sequel is titled *I'll Be There*.

Gibbons, Kaye. *Ellen Foster.* This is a little gem of a book about a young southern girl whose parents die. The main character is so plucky and without self-pity that the reader loves her. My students with fairly good reading skills enjoy this book; those with mediocre or poor skills find it confusing and boring.

Golding, William. My average-reading boys enjoy *Lord of the Flies*, which is about a group of boys who become savages when stranded on a desert island. "Very good book. Fierce growing up experience is demonstrated in an exaggerated way and made believable."

Guest, Judith. *Ordinary People.* This book is a little confusing at first. You might explain to your teenager that the chapters are written in a stream-of-consciousness style, and the focus switches between Conrad and his father. "About the Jarretts, a family who lost one of their two sons in a sailing accident. At the end the emotion was so strong I cried. Because of the strong emotion, it makes the book intense, hard to put down. I wanted to read more and so I did a lot of reading. Only problem is that it's going to be a hard book to follow." It's true. Students enjoy Guest's next book, *Second Heaven*, but they don't love it like *Ordinary People*.

Irving, John. *The World According to Garp.* High school athletes, especially, love the book because the main character is first a wrestler, and then becomes a wrestling coach. His books are tragic-comic, and demand a thoughtful reader, but not one with especially sophisticated reading skills. Some of the subject matter is pretty adult, however; don't give his books to young kids. Other popular titles: *Hotel New Hampshire, Cider House Rules, A Prayer for Owen Meany*.

Knowles, John. *A Separate Peace.* A teenager should be thoughtful, perceptive, and have fairly good reading skills to enjoy this book. "Two kids in their senior year of high school getting ready to be drafted into WWII. A great book, sentimental and touching." His sequel, *Peace Breaks Out*, is not nearly as popular.

*Lee, Harper. *To Kill a Mockingbird.* An almost infallible book for a teenager with at least low to average reading skills. "Marvelous, a page-turner. Life and times of young girl and family growing up in an old-fashioned and prejudiced community. Shows the incredible love that holds her family together. Contains scenes which will make you laugh and scenes that will make you cry."

McMillan, Terry. *Waiting to Exhale.* This is a novel about four African-American women who are frustrated by their inability to find suitable African-American men. My students are just discovering this book, and so far all of the reports have been positive.

Pilcher, Rosamunde. Her books swept my British Literature class this spring. A couple of students read almost every one. She's a Danielle Steel who's more realistic. "Her books are set in England and are about love and family problems." My students advise each other to start with her older, shorter novels, like *The Empty House, Under Gemini, The End of Summer, Carousel, Another View, Snow in April,* and *Voices in Summer. The Shell Seekers*, her best-known book, they comment, is "long, don't read first."

Salinger, J. D. *Catcher in the Rye.* High school students having at least moderate reading skills and a somewhat nontraditional view of life are most likely to enjoy this. "Shows that looks can be deceiving. Holden, who in the eyes of others appears to be a messed-up kid, is really a sensitive boy. Also, the book was written in a personal friend-to-friend style that I found to be easy and relaxing." Salinger's other books aren't as popular with my students now as I remember them being twenty years ago, but they are still read. In decreasing order of popularity: *Nine Stories, Franny and Zooey,* and *Raise High the Roof Beam, Carpenters and Seymour: an Introduction.*

Segal, Erich. *Love Story* remains very popular, and is easy enough for junior high girls or very poor high school readers. "A quick comforting book. Good holiday read." My students find *Oliver's Story* okay, but not wonderful. They find *Man, Woman, and Child* better than *Oliver's Story,* but not as good as *Love Story.* His more recent titles include *The Class, Doctors,* and *Acts of Faith.*

*Steel, Danielle. Wonderful books for teenage girls who don't think they like reading, or even those who do like reading. *The Promise* is a good one to start with because it's short. "I like this book a lot. I haven't really liked a book in awhile." Another girl: "I have never read so much so fast." Some other favorites: *Star:* "The best. I loved this book." *Palomino:* "Woman's husband leaves her so she goes to a ranch to forget. Characters and situations seem so life-like that it's almost like I can put myself in Samantha's shoes and feel exactly what she's feeling. This happens to me in all of Danielle Steel's books." *Fine Things:* "About this businessman who marries this schoolteacher. She finds out she has cancer and this is extremely sad. I cried a lot. I find myself wanting to continue to read on. I've read so much at night lately." *Daddy:* "I cried all the way through it."

Tyler, Anne. Tyler writes what might be called adult coming-of-age books. Her style is not difficult but the kinds of characters she creates require a mature reader. I don't think I've ever seen a student under the age of fifteen enjoy any of her books. But the right older reader may love her. Best bet: *The Accidental Tourist:* "It's seldom that I find a book I don't want to put down, but I've definitely found one. Macon's crazy ideas and inventions are hilarious." Other ones to try: *Searching for Caleb, Morgan's Passing.*

HISTORICAL OR POLITICAL AUTHORS

JUVENILE AUTHORS
Lovelace, Maud Hart. Betsy-Tacy books, a turn-of-the-century coming-of-age series. First two titles: *Betsy-Tacy* and *Betsy, Tacy and Tib.* "Showed what it was like to live in 1904. Showed what they did for fun." These were my own favorite books growing up, and I was really surprised and delighted to see that a fair number of my students had also discovered these books and fallen in love with them. "We used to play Betsy-Tacy at recess." The first six books of this series are out in paperback, but you have to search libraries for the last two books of the high school series, and the books about Betsy's job and marriage. This is an interesting series because the style and plots become more sophisticated as Betsy grows up; the early books are appropriate for early elementary school kids, and the last books are fine for junior high and high school kids.

Montgomery, L. M. Anne of Green Gables books. First two titles: *Anne of Green Gables, Anne of Avonlea.* About an orphan coming to Prince Edward Island during the turn of the century. These books require a fairly sophisticated reader, and only my best readers reported enjoying them in elementary school. But the ones who read them really loved them. "I've read them all at least twice." Some of my high school students discovered these books, and read them for the first time as eleventh- or twelfth-graders. Try to keep your children away from the PBS television series until after they've read the books. The PBS series is done so well— and the books are written in such a leisurely style—that all but my best readers become impatient with the books after seeing the series.

Wilder, Laura Ingalls. Little House books. First two titles: *Little House in the Big Woods, Little House on the Prairie.* These books, which are written in a very simple, accessible style, are about the joys and sorrows of a nineteenth-century American family. Excellent for an elementary school girl who's just starting to read independently. Many, many of my students remember loving this series. "Good to learn history in a fun way. Learn how people grew up back then and how you had to live without TV." Another student said simply: "Will always be my favorite."

ADULT TITLES
Auel, Jean M. *The Clan of the Cave Bear.* This story, which assumes the possibility that humans evolved in two separate strains, one of which died out, describes the life of an orphan girl, of our strain of evolution, who is raised by a tribe of the other evolutionary strain. This first book, which I understand is grounded in solid academic theory, is very interesting for a number of my high school students. "Fascinating," commented one. Parents should be aware that the later titles, such as *The Valley of the Horses, The Plains of Passage,* and *The Mammoth Hunters* have a number of sexually explicit scenes. Not for young kids, certainly.

Austen, Jane. *Pride and Prejudice.* Only give this late eighteenth-century novel to kids with excellent reading skills. Some boys enjoy the satire, but many girls simply fall in love with the romance in the book, and read it over and over again. "A story of Pride and Prejudice going against each other. It teaches you to loosen our pride and to judge people by yourself. This story is a treasure I cannot possibly let go." Some of my students liked *Pride and Prejudice* so much that they wanted to read Austen's other books. *Emma* was the only one they liked at all, although one girl did enjoy *Sense and Sensibility*. I loved the BBC television productions of her books, but the class laughed at me and said they looked like they were done with a home camcorder.

Brontë, Charlotte, *Jane Eyre.* A nineteenth-century or-phan-finds-happiness story. A number of students are assigned this book to read in ninth grade, and many report to me that they didn't like it. The girls who weren't assigned the novel in ninth grade usually choose to read it as a junior in British Literature and *love* it. I'm not sure if the extra two years maturity make the difference—or if choosing this book oneself is necessary to enjoying it. Many of my British Literature kids try *Wuthering Heights* by Emily Brontë next, but are invariably disappointed. They don't like it nearly as well as *Jane Eyre.*

Fitzgerald, F. Scott. *The Great Gatsby.* A deceptively sim-ple book about life in the jazz age. The reader doesn't need sophisticated reading skills, but does need to be thoughtful and perceptive about life to enjoy the book. "The story of a man named Jay Gatsby and his relationships with other people told through the narrator, Nick Carroway. This novel is very short and to the point, but also very absorbing." I've had students try his other novels, but they don't like them as well.

Heller, Joseph. *Catch-22.* A World War II book only for sophisticated readers. "I couldn't put it down . . . it really pulled me into its enormously strange, exaggerated, and unique world. I think the way everyone should read this in order to avoid confusion is to read it but not pay complete attention to it. If somebody does that there is no doubt they will get lost. You have to let the book settle and explain itself. All of a sudden it will all make sense."

Hemingway, Ernest. Most of his books are set in the early twentieth century. Younger students find him boring, but thoughtful older students (at least fifteen, I'd guess) find some of his books rewarding. *The Old Man and the Sea:* "I am finding it incredibly enjoyable. What I find most interesting so far is the old man's determination and how he still goes out and doesn't get overwhelmed or discouraged by not catching anything for so long." Other titles for older students: *The Sun Also Rises:* "So simple and very descriptive. His writing style is very beautiful." *A Farewell to Arms:* "The plot is intriguing, the characters endearing. The descriptions? I loved them."

Kesey, Ken. *One Flew over the Cuckoo's Nest.* This book is narrated by an Indian chief whose mental state fades in and out of reality. This unreliable narrator makes it confusing but also very funny. Above average reading skills are needed to enjoy it. "The story of a loud, boisterous convict and his fight against the tyrannical nurse in the ward of a mental hospital. A very good statement against people who abuse their power. It shows how people need to be treated as human beings, not children. A ten!" There's a wonderful movie of it, but wait until your teen has finished the book.

L'Amour, Louis. A writer of historical fiction, usually westerns, who prided himself on the accuracy of his historical detail. *The Walking Drum* is set in twelfth-century Asia. "A spectacular book! Probably Louis L'Amour's greatest! ... Did you know that the Christian religion believed that bathing was a sin? One nun even bragged that she hadn't bathed in sixty-five years! Bathing was introduced by the

Greeks and the Muslims." Other favorite L'Amour titles: *The Lonesome Gods, Reilly's Luck, Sackett, Sackett's Land,* and *Jubal Sackett.*

Mitchell, Margaret. *Gone With the Wind.* Girls today love this book as much as ever.

Plaidy, Jean. Writes historical novels about the English, Scottish, and French monarchies. I have had a couple of students who were fantastic readers read everything she wrote (which is *considerable*). But kids don't need to be excellent readers to enjoy her. She's very accessible, plus the kids learn a good deal of history. Writes romantic suspense under the name of Victoria Holt. You can get the Holt titles (see Mystery section) in bookstores, but you pretty much need to get the Plaidy titles through a library. Some Plaidy titles: *The Bastard King, The Captive Queen of Scots, The Courts of Love, The Follies of the King, It Began in Vauxhall Gardens, Murder Most Royal.*

Orwell, George. *Animal Farm.* A good book for average readers who want to read something intellectual and important. "The hidden reality of communism in a farm was an appealing trait for me to read about." Or for students who like animals: "I love this book. I am an animal rights fanatic so I think this book is great."

Remarque, Erich Maria. *All Quiet on the Western Front.* The must book for the student with above-average reading skills and an interest in history. "About a German soldier during World War I. A wonderful book. It is upsetting and sad, but it gives the reader a sense of understanding just what the soldiers went through. At the same time, it makes war itself seem completely incomprehensible."

Rice, Anne. For sophisticated readers. Kids who've already read a fair amount of fantasy or horror and who enjoy history seem to do best with her. The Vampire books (*Interview with the Vampire, The Vampire Lestat, The Queen of the Damned,* and *The Tale of the Body Thief*) take the reader across centuries. You're in the mind of very complicated, sophisticated vampires. "Horrifying romances set in a gothic scene. Louis and Lestat must learn to live a life of constant betrayal to keep their status as vampires. It hurts the men in the end—they have no one to turn to—only each other for comfort." *The Feasts of All Saints:* Set in New Orleans right before the Civil War. Describes the society of free Mulattos and Quadroons. "Good historical novel. One of her best." *The Mummy, or Ramses the Damned:* "Interesting because the characters were real (Ramses and Cleopatra) but set in a fictional way. Told a lot about the Egyptians and how they lived."

Steinbeck, John. *Of Mice and Men.* Excellent, short book for average to poor readers who must read a classic for school. "About two guys, George and Lennie. Lennie is retarded. Every job they get is ruined when Lennie does something wrong in his ignorance. I totally cried at the end of that book. It was so sad. Everyone liked it." Better readers love *East of Eden*, a family saga set in the first part of the twentieth century. Although this book is very long, most kids with average to above average reading skills love it. By far this is the most popular Steinbeck book. "I loved this book. I read every page. I couldn't put it down. At first the number of pages threw me but I really loved this book." Every year it sweeps my American Literature classes. "This book is great. There is tons of gruesome stuff. I didn't think Steinbeck had it in him. Plus, he's so descriptive it seems like it's happening outside your door." As for Steinbeck's other most popular books, kids find *The Red Pony, The Pearl,* and *The Grapes of Wrath* engrossing but depressing. Very good readers will like *Cannery Row, Sweet Thursday,* and *Tor-*

tilla Flat, but mediocre readers find them confusing and pointless.

Uris, Leon. Historical fiction that boys, especially, seem to do well with. *Exodus:* "I would have to say that this is probably the best book I have ever read. For the past four weeks this book has almost controlled my life. I found myself sneaking it to places where I was not supposed to be reading it, because I was at a very exciting part." *Trinity:* "I was getting too involved. I was going to only want to read and neglect the rest of my life."

Vonnegut, Kurt. Somewhat dated, but some students still love his offbeat, satiric portrayals. Favorite titles: *Player Piano, Cat's Cradle,* and *Slaughter House Five,* which is a description of the firebombing of Dresden with an odd, fantasy interval thrown in. *Welcome to the Monkey House,* a book of some of his early short stories, is good because, as one student said, "Vonnegut thinks in short stories." The student added, "As time went on, so did Vonnegut's ability to control his wandering mind. His later books really lose coherency. *Slapstick* and *Galapagos* are the best of the worst."

Walker, Alice. *The Color Purple.* Most of my high school girls, with at least average reading skills, love this story of Celie, a poor black girl who survives an abusive home and marriage and triumphs in the end. It's set during the early part of the twentieth century, and is written in the form of letters. For young African-American women, I think this book is a must try. They'll almost certainly love it.

Walker, Margaret. *Jubilee.* "Story of a girl whose mother was a slave and her father was a master. About her struggle for freedom. Long, and you have to concentrate to keep up with the characters." Another must try for African-American students.

Waugh, Evelyn. His satiric pictures of the British upper class call for a sophisticated reader. *A Handful of Dust, Decline and Fall, Brideshead Revisited.* "His books' titles describe the crumbling facade of upper class morality, and one can picture Evelyn standing in front of this with a sledgehammer."

Woodiwiss, Kathleen. *The Flame and the Flower, The Wolf and the Dove.* These are wonderful "trashy" historical romances that show girls aged thirteen on up that books are *much* more interesting than television or movies. They have a bit of sex, but I think they're essentially harmless. And your daughter might even learn a little history!

MYSTERY AND HORROR

JUVENILE AUTHORS
*Bellairs, John. Wrote *many* titles. A small sample: *Chessman of Doom, The Curse of the Blue Figurine, The Dark Secret of Weatherend, The Eyes of the Killer Robot, The House with a Clock in Its Walls, The Letter, the Witch, and the Ring.* His books tend toward ghost and horror stories, sometimes with magic. "Best books. Gave me nightmares but I always read them."

CHOOSE YOUR OWN ADVENTURE books. These books offer the reader choices about story endings. The reader will get to a thrilling point in the plot and be given a choice as to what the main character should do. What pages the reader reads next depends on his or her decision. These are a good bridge between picture books and longer chapter books. They were the entry into independent reading for my younger daughter. Occasionally, they have been the only books I've been able to get my very low-reading sophomores to read. These books make the reader feel part of the action: "And then it says I could go into the cave, or keep on down the trail. I choose the cave because . . . " Although different authors write Choose Your Own Adventure books, they are usually shelved together in the bookstore. Libraries shelve them by author. Some of the more prolific authors and a sampling of their books: Richard Brightfield: *The Dragon's Den, Master of Karate, Planet of the Dragons, Hijacked.* Louise M. Foley: *Danger at Anchor Mine.* Shannon Gilligan: *The Case of the Silk King, The Terrorist Trap.* Jay Leibold: *Beyond the Great Wall, Fight for Freedom, Return of the Ninja.* R. A. Montgomery: *Blood on the Handle, Caravan, The Island of Time, Silver Wings.* Edward Packard: *Kidnapped, Superbike.*

*Dixon, Franklin W. The Hardy Boys books have been around for decades, and they are still wonderful for getting third- through fifth- or sixth-grade boys reading. The Hardys are two teenage brothers who solve mysteries. "Good. First books I really liked. I read all I could find."

*Duncan, Lois. Young Adult writer. Very, very popular books for late elementary, junior high, and early high school readers. Some favorites: *Stranger with My Face:* "About twins who got separated at birth." *A Gift of Magic:* "I really liked it because I had an interest in ESP when I was young. Told a lot of the problems it can cause, and the advantages of it." *I Know What You Did Last Summer:* "Easy to relate to because the kids were around our age." Other popular titles: *Killing Mr. Griffin, Summer of Fear, The Third Eye,* and *Don't Look Behind You.*

Estes, Rose. The Three Investigators series. Sample titles: *The Three Investigators in the Case of the Dancing Dinosaur, The Three Investigators in the Case of the House of Horrors.* Again, this was one of the few nonfantasy series that boys seem to enjoy. "I loved the mystery and trying to figure out how the crime was being solved. I was always wrong, but it was fun to see how good friends could be so together in solving mysteries. I used to read them on the bus to school in third and fourth grade."

Fitzgerald, John D. The Great Brain series. Sample titles: *The Great Brain at the Academy, The Great Brain Does It Again.* A number of boys mentioned this series as one of the few they enjoyed around third or fourth grade. "Wicked good."

Fitzhugh, Louise. *Harriet the Spy.* A sixth-grade girl is determined to be a famous author, and so writes what she sees every day. Unfortunately, someone finds her notebook. Sequel: *The Long Secret.*

Hass, E. A. *Incognito Mosquito, Private Insective; Incognito Mosquito Flies Again; Incognito Mosquito Makes History!; Incognito Mosquito Takes to the Air.* Short, illustrated mysteries for kids just starting to read independently. "A whole series. Great books!"

*Keene, Carolyn. The Nancy Drew books are another venerable series, the female version of the Hardy Boys. Sample titles: *The Bungalow Mystery, The Clue in the Diary.* "I loved those books! I still read them. Really good mysteries. I don't like any other kind of mysteries. Some of them are really creepy. They really stump you. I still love them so much. Newer ones are easier to understand but I liked the old ones better. Had more substance to them. The newer ones were more airheaded."

Langton, Jane. *The Diamond in the Window.* "Takes place in Concord. Deals with two children who have to follow a treasure hunt. I liked it a lot; my brothers did too." Easy reading.

Stine, R. L. Has written many Young Adult mysteries. A few titles: *Halloween Party, Lights Out, The Secret Bedroom, Ski*

Weekend, The Sleepwalker, The Wrong Number. "My friend and I set an hour a day to read *The Wrong Number* aloud to each other. I've never had more fun reading in my life. It's like we're in a movie!"

Warner, Gertrude. The Boxcar Children series. Four orphans make a home in a boxcar and, as the series progresses, find a home with their grandfather. Easy mysteries. Elementary school age. My high school students tell me their little brothers and sisters like these.

ADULT MYSTERIES AND HORROR

Christie, Agatha. A student needs pretty sophisticated reading skills to enjoy her mysteries. But those students love her. "*Easy to Kill* was shocking and tragic. Very suspenseful. You would never suspect who ended up doing the murder." *The Murder of Roger Ackroyd:* "I enjoyed it a lot but was upset at who the murderer was." Christie's short stories don't work well with even good readers, but the following mysteries usually do: *The A.B.C. Murders, And Then There Were None, The Body in the Library, A Caribbean Mystery, Cat Among the Pigeons, Curtain, Death on the Nile, Endless Night, Evil under the Sun, The Mirror Crack'd, Mrs. McGinty's Dead, A Murder Is Announced, Murder on the Orient Express, A Pocket Full of Rye, Third Girl,* and *What Mrs. McGillicuddy Saw!*

*Clark, Mary Higgins. Pure suspense. The reader watches innocent people being stalked. "Her books were what really motivated me to read." Point of view shifts, which makes them a little more difficult to read than Robert Parker's Spenser mysteries, but if kids can follow the books they can't put them down. *While My Pretty One Sleeps:* "Writer friend gets killed and girl tries to solve the mystery. Really good. Five stars!" *All Around the Town:* "Sister gets kidnapped when she's a kid. Has multiple personalities.

Gets charged for a murder she couldn't do. Five stars!" *A Cry in the Night:* "Divorced woman meets and marries an artist, begins to realize there is something strange about her husband's ways. I haven't read any books that contain characters like these ones. The only resemblance I can find is the 'trapped' feeling the female figure has which can be compared to some of V. C. Andrews' characters. It's books like this that make reading worthwhile." Other favorite titles: *The Cradle Will Fall, Stillwatch, A Stranger Is Watching, Weep No More My Lady, Where Are the Children?*

Cook, Robin. Cook, a doctor, writes highly suspenseful novels with medical settings. Readers watch victims being stalked and killed, often by doctors. He uses a great deal of medical technology; kids interested in science or medicine seem to do the best with these. *Coma:* "Stephen King gone high-tech in a hospital world. The best. Five stars!" Other favorites: *Brain, Mutation, Fever, Outbreak, Mindbend, Godplayer, Blindsight,* and *Mutation.*

Crichton, Michael. *Jurassic Park.* This suspense novel was originally assigned by a science teacher as part of an earth science course. So many students loved the book that now word has spread and it's sweeping the school. Try it for moderate readers who are interested in science (anything to do with dinosaurs, especially!).

Du Maurier, Daphne. *Rebecca* is an almost infallible book for a high school girl with at least average reading skills. "The story of a newlywed girl and her 'battle' with her husband's dead wife. An absolutely incredible book. When reading *Rebecca* I found myself becoming more and more ambitious for the next page, the next sentence, even the next word." Students often try to find another book of du Maurier's that's as good, but can't. *My Cousin Rachel* comes the closest.

Francis, Dick. Francis uses first-person narrators, which make his novels easier to follow, but they still seem to demand a fairly good reader to be enjoyed. His thrillers combine mystery and suspense, and always have something to do with horse racing. *Flying Finish:* "The plot is wonderful but simple, and the suspense is amazing." "I loved *In the Frame.*" *Proof:* "I love the book. It was one of my favorites, not too much violence, just a few dead bodies. As usual, it kept me reading throughout." *For Kicks:* "One of his best." The nice thing about Francis's books is that he's such an even writer that all his books are good. You don't have to be careful when picking titles.

Grafton, Sue. Her mysteries about a female investigator all have titles beginning with a letter of the alphabet. *A Is for Alibi, B Is for Burglar,* up to, so far, *I Is for Innocent.* "Lead character is a woman. Different from the normal mysteries because she leads a different life. Interesting because she's smart and knows what to do. The plots aren't deep so you don't have to get into it."

*Grisham, John. A new author who's taking my classes by storm. His suspense novels have a lawyer as the main character. *The Firm:* "My mind tends to wander when I read, but not during this book. My whole family was talking about how wonderful it was, and so I had to read it." *A Time to Kill:* "Really blew me away . . . deals with some serious moral dilemmas that face this country." *The Pelican Brief* is a bit more complicated, but equally suspenseful. His newest book is *The Client.*

Harris, Thomas. Kids are fascinated by psychopathic killers, like Harris's Lecter, but need slightly better than average reading skills or they get bogged down. "*The Silence of the Lambs* was scary. Only book I've ever been afraid of. Dealt with completely innocent people getting massacred."

The Red Dragon: "Very exciting and gross. A ten. I loved it!" Because these books are so powerful and scary, you should probably only give them to older kids who don't get nightmares.

Hillerman, Tony. Easy to follow mysteries set in the Southwest that feature a Navajo detective. "The Navajo detective does things by Indian methods, like looking for tracks." Some favorite titles: *The Dark Wind, Listening Woman, Skinwalkers,* and *Talking God.*

Holt, Victoria. Writes romantic suspense. My kids are just starting to discover her. *Bride of Pendorric:* "Young woman needs to find out if she can trust her husband. Excellent." *The Judas Kiss:* "A romance/mystery novel about two young girls whose parents die so they are forced to live with their grandfather. He appears to be incredibly cruel. As always, Victoria Holt kept my interest up to the highest degree." Other titles: *The Silk Vendetta, The Captive, Daughter of Deceit.*

Kellerman, Jonathan. His mysteries feature a psychiatrist as his detective. Pretty good readers, especially those interested in psychiatry, really enjoy him. *Over the Edge:* "About a psychiatrist from one of his former patients. I loved this book. I thought it was really good. That's why I read so much. I couldn't put it down." Other titles: *Private Eyes, Silent Partner, When the Bough Breaks.*

Kemelman, Harry. The Rabbi Small series. Some of my students are just discovering him, and are really enjoying his gentle, comic descriptions of life and murder in a small New England town. First title: *Friday the Rabbi Slept Late.*

*King, Stephen. King should get a gold medal for helping so many young people love reading. All of his books (except, possibly, *The Eyes of the Dragon*) work well. Some favorites:

Night Shift: "A series of short stories. A lot of them are sort of preludes to his other books. These stories are really scary. They actually gave me nightmares and I don't scare easily." *The Stand:* "Intertwines fantasy and the surreal. Often I found myself believing in the evil character 'The Dark Man' unhesitatingly, and when I put the book down found myself peering fearfully around the room. An excellent book. Stephen King always surprises me with his incredible power with words." *The Shining:* "The book got so interesting that I read over one hundred and fifty pages in one week, three times what I normally read. A psychological thriller as well as a horror story." Less competent readers enjoy his short stories in *Night Shift,* or *Different Seasons.* A short novel in *Four Past Midnight, The Langoliers,* got one of my hardest kids reading. It's a story about eight or nine people who fall asleep on a plane, and when they wake up, everyone else is gone. "All that are left on the seats are jewelry and tooth fillings."

Koontz, Dean R. Teenage boys, especially, seem to enjoy his books after they've exhausted Stephen King. "*Midnight* was really weird. People go back and regress into animalistic forms that kill people who were trying to become better in the name of progress. It grabbed you. Intellectually stimulating." *The Voice of the Night:* "Two fourteen-year-old boys are friends, one popular, good looking, the other a loser, nerd. Quick reading, easy to relate to, all around much better than the other books by Koontz I have read." *Nightfall:* "A voodoo priest is killing off a mafia's family for revenge and to please the gods. A great chase through all of New York City!" *Lightning:* "A lot of subplots. Hard to figure out. He keeps you reading. There are hardly any slow parts."

Langton, Jane. *Emily Dickinson Is Dead.* The story takes place in Amherst, Massachusetts at the centennial commemoration of Dickinson's death. "Arson, murder, and forgery are connected with the story. I'd really recommend it."

*Parker, Robert B. His Spenser series, about a private detective, is set in Boston. Funny first-person narrator makes the action really easy to follow. I've watched many students fall in love with reading with these books. "Once you start on Parker you can't stop." A number of my students confided to me that these were the first books they'd ever really finished. *Early Autumn:* "About a kid. Liked how it was so realistic and how the parents treated the boy— used one against the other. I don't really read books that often, but I can see myself continuing in the series." Another young man said about *Early Autumn*, "This is the first book I have ever had *any* desire to read." *Crimson Joy:* "Five Stars! Suspenseful. Real mystery! Serial killer in Boston who leaves a rose on his victims. Easily the best book I've read." *A Catskill Eagle:* "Liked it a lot. One of his best." *Stardust:* "Movie star getting crank calls. It got my attention more than any other book." Other favorite titles: *Pastime, Playmates, Ceremony, Double Deuce, Pale Kings and Princes, God Save the Child, The Judas Goat, Looking for Rachel Wallace, Mortal Stakes, Taming a Sea-Horse.*

Paretsky, Sara. The V. I. Warshawski mysteries. These feature a female private eye. "Really good, fast moving, interesting. Sometimes you know who the bad guy is; sometimes you don't. A lot like the Sue Grafton mysteries." Some titles: *Bitter Medicine, Blood Shot, Guardian Angel.*

Peretti, Frank E. Peretti is a Christian writer (and sometimes only available in Christian bookstores) who adds a moral dimension to his suspense tales by dealing with such issues as abortion. "About how spirits affect earth. Any book. They can keep you up for hours." Favorites: The

Darkness series (*This Present Darkness, Piercing the Darkness*) and *Tilly*.

Sandford, John. Sandford's books swept my mystery elective. The easiest to read is his first one, *Rules of Prey*. "Maddog killer who left notes describing 'rules' like never kill anyone you know. It was cool. Psycho killer." Four sequels so far: *Shadow Prey, Eyes of Prey, Silent Prey*, and *Winter Prey*, all of which feature the same detective, Lieutenant Davenport. If you've despaired of ever having your high school son finish a book, these might be the first ones he can't put down. Be aware, however, that they are pretty gory, and shouldn't be given to younger children or nightmare-prone teenagers.

Sheldon, Sidney. Average reading skills are fine for these. Sheldon seems to be especially good for bright girls who just don't read much. "*Master of the Game* is a novel which would be classified as trashy, but is interesting and makes you want to read; that is, if you like melodrama. It is about a girl who grows up to become a very powerful businesswoman, who denies her family for power." "*The Other Side of Midnight* is a mysterious tragedy. It's really long, but I couldn't put it down." Other favorites: *If Tomorrow Comes, The Naked Face, Rage of Angels*, and *A Stranger in the Mirror*. "Sheldon's books are really gripping, and they are really hard to put down."

Turow, Scott. *Presumed Innocent* needs a fast reader because the first half of the book is pretty slow. But some fast readers love it: "Good mystery. Interesting with the trial and the way the defense is planned." His second book, *The Burden of Proof*, is equally popular with fast readers.

Westlake, Donald E. Every so often a boy with only average reading skills discovers Donald Westlake, and falls in love with his books. Good readers love his tragic-comic, incompetent characters too. His caper mysteries are both funny and suspenseful. Try some of his older titles first; kids seem to like them better. Best bets: *God Save the Mark; Help! I Am Being Held Prisoner; The Hot Rock.*

Whitney, Phyllis. She's written many novels of romantic suspense, but my readers recommend her more current ones, such as *Dream of Orchids, The Ebony Swan, Feather on the Moon, The Flaming Tree, Poinciana, Rainbow in the Mist, Sea Jade, Silversword, The Singing Stones.*

ESPIONAGE AND WAR AUTHORS

Clancy, Tom. His international thrillers are full of accurate military detail; boys love them. Excellent reading skills aren't as important as an interest in the military. I think his first one, *The Hunt for Red October,* is his best and most accessible, but I have students who love them all. *Patriot Games:* "A very good story! It was sometimes hard to understand all the high-tech stuff, but it was a good look at terrorism and the life of terrorists. Action! Adventure! High body count!" *The Sum of All Fears:* "It is like his other novels, suspenseful, you cannot stop reading it . . . full of action and violence, also very good and interesting." *Red Storm Rising:* "Keeps the reader tied to a chair frantically reading to find new info." Other favorites: *Clear and Present Danger* and *The Cardinal of the Kremlin.*

Cussler, Clive. Writes espionage adventure books. Some of my average to good reading tenth- through twelfth-grade boys are big fans. Favorites: *Deep Six, Iceberg, Mediterranean Caper,* and *Dragon:* "His books always have something lost, something secret only highest levels know. Other people look to get them and destroy before the Americans can. Earlier books are better." His newest is *Sahara.*

Follett, Ken. Espionage writer. *Eye of the Needle, The Key to Rebecca, The Man from St. Petersburg.* He does have one historical thriller that is a favorite of my students, *Pillars of the Earth.* "About the Middle Ages. About four central characters, a mason, a prior, another mason, and a noble woman. Long, about a thousand pages, but really good. I never read much until I read this. Ever since then I've been somewhat of a busy reader." His most recent title is *Night over Water.*

Griffin, W. E. His Brotherhood of War series, which my students are just discovering, and really love. Great books for boys. *The Lieutenants:* "It's really good. I like old war movies and this reads a lot like an old WWII movie. There are all the classic elements of a good war story: Americans versus Nazis, prison camps, tanks, planes, etc." The books are about the army, and follow the careers of several people, mostly officers, through WWII, Korea, and Vietnam. Other series: The Corps and Badge of Honor.

LeCarré, John. His dark novels of espionage are only for very sophisticated readers; he's difficult but a number of my British Literature students really enjoyed him. The titles include *The Spy Who Came in from the Cold; Tinker, Tailor, Soldier, Spy; Smiley's People.* "Smiley's wonderful. He makes a great twentieth-century protagonist, in that he's an individual caught in the huge gears of the modern world, which appear to be turning just for the sake of turning. LeCarré makes him real to me by tangling his personal life with his career, and making all his doubts and worries so down to earth. I enjoyed these books muchly."

Ludlum, Robert. Another good writer for boys. One boy, who didn't usually read very much, told me that he had spent so much time reading his first Ludlum that he didn't know if he wanted to read another. "They take too much of my time. I don't do anything else." Of course, I handed him the next one and said, "Read it!" *The Bourne Identity:* "A man with incredible talents is pulled from the ocean with amnesia. The plot is so head-spinning and mind-blowing that you really can't put the book down." *Trevayne:* "About a man who is chosen by the president to head up a subcommittee to find out the wrongdoings of the defense department. A wonderful suspense novel filled with intrigue and excitement." Other favorites: *The Scarlatti Inheritance, The Bourne Supremacy, The Bourne Ultimatum, The Matarese Circle, The Aquitaine Progression.*

MacLean, Alistair. A British author. When I finally allow my British Literature class to read contemporary writers, the boys flock to MacLean. Some favorites: *Athabasca, Circus, Ice Station Zebra, Partisans, Puppet on a Chain, Santorini.*

Michener, James. Kids like his books once they get into them. Tell them it's perfectly okay to skip his long opening chapters, which sometimes deal with prehistory going back to volcanoes and earth formations. One student told me that *Space* was the easiest to get into. Other titles: *Hawaii* and *The Source.*

SCIENCE FICTION AND FANTASY

JUVENILE AUTHORS
Alexander, Lloyd. Many high school fantasy readers report starting with him. His novels include *The Book of Three* and *The Black Cauldron.* "A coming-of-age type story. Kid whose quest is to find his father. Gets involved with prince and has to stop powerful wizard who tries to take over the world with a zombie army." Again, this is another author best for fairly competent readers. Many of my very good readers remember his books with affection.

Banks, Lynn Reid. *The Indian in the Cupboard, The Return of the Indian, The Secret of the Indian.* "About a boy who gets a plastic toy Indian. He puts it in a cupboard and locks it. The Indian comes to life and goes on adventures." These are great elementary school books, especially good for children who like stories about dolls or toys that come to life. Banks has written many other books, but these are her most popular.

Cooper, Susan. She writes a fairly sophisticated fantasy series that deals with the King Arthur legends. Many of my best readers remember loving her books. Titles, in order: *Over Sea, Under Stone; The Dark Is Rising; Greenwitch, The Grey King; Silver on the Tree.*

Jacques, Brian. The Redwall series. Titles: *Mossflower, Redwall, Mattimeo,* and *Mariel of Mossflower.* "About an abbey of mice who are very peaceful and try to keep a rat named Cluny the Scourge from taking over the abbey. Books have a lot of suspense—you can't predict what will happen. Exciting and funny. Like a comic fairy tale. They leave you feeling contented."

L'Engle, Madeleine. Sample titles: *A Swiftly Tilting Planet, A Wind in the Door, Meet the Austins, The Young Unicorns.* She writes fairly complex fantasy for late elementary school and middle school kids. Don't give her books to a mediocre reader because they can be confusing. But some good readers really love her. *A Wrinkle in Time* is the book most often mentioned. "I loved that book. I've read it five times." Also popular is *Many Waters.* "A kid's transported back in time to the time of Noah. Weird. Different. I just liked it."

Lewis, C. S. The Chronicles of Narnia. First titles in series of nine: *The Lion, the Witch, and the Wardrobe; Prince Caspian.* These books are wonderful for getting kids interested in fantasy. Another must try for boys, although one of my daughters loved them too. "Awesome books. Has Snow Queen and Aslan the lion. Shows lions aren't always beasts. Kids have to go on all these adventures, save things in Narnia. Hard to explain but really good. When we were eight or nine we used to pretend we were magic horses and we used to play Narnia."

Yolen, Jane. The Pit Dragon Trilogy, which includes *Dragon's Blood, Heart's Blood,* and *A Sending of Dragons.* This trilogy describes Jakkin, a young Pit Master training fighting dragons on the Planet Austar IV. Excellent fantasy books for late elementary or junior high students. "Great fantasy writer."

ADULT AUTHORS
Adams, Douglas. Hitchhikers' Guide series. Fairly easy to read books that boys, especially, seem to enjoy. "Hysterically funny, amazingly witty and clever, and generally fantastic." First title: *The Hitchhiker's Guide to the Galaxy.* "I hadn't read *Hitchhiker's* since middle school, and I wanted to read it again with my abundant wealth of worldly insights I have gained since then. It was just as funny and plotless as I remembered it." Other titles: *The Restaurant at the End of the Universe; So Long, and Thanks for all the Fish; Life, the Universe, and Everything; Mostly Harmless.* The Hitcher's series is a comic, harmless spoof on science fiction.

*Anthony, Piers. He's a very prolific writer, but his Xanth series is the best to start with. Countless students of mine have fallen in love with fantasy, and reading in general, with these books about a land where magic is commonplace. "The best. Really weird, funny." The series starts with *A Spell for Chameleon,* and continues on through many more books, which should be read in order. Tell your child to skip the first two or three pages in *A Spell for Chameleon,* which are difficult, boring, and irrelevant to the rest of the story. Then he or she should really enjoy it. "Exciting . . . good detail." This series is a must try for boys who don't think they like reading: "His imagery is wonderful, rich, and beautiful. Piers Anthony brings his fictional world alive better than most authors I've read." Other series: The Apprentice Adept, Cluster, and Incantations of Immortality.

Asimov, Isaac. Fairly difficult science fiction, but a real favorite of some of my better-reading boys. *I, Robot:* "His best. The life of a robot. Set the standard for robot novels with his prime directives for robots." Asimov has written many science fiction novels (and many books of other genres), but my science fiction fans tell me that his Foundation Trilogy, which consists of *Foundation, Second Foundation,* and *Foundation and Empire* is the best. It is preceded by *Prelude to Foundation.*

Asprin, Robert. *Another Fine Myth.* This is the first book in his very funny Myth series. These books are short, quickly read, and perfect for that junior high or high school boy you're trying to move to books. "Just a fun author to read, along the lines of Piers Anthony, but more into humor." Next two titles in the Myth series: *Myth Conceptions, Myth Directions.* He has a new series now called Phule's Company.

Bradbury, Ray. Bradbury is one of the earlier writers in the science fiction field, but competent teenage readers still enjoy his books. "If you're not a good reader you're just going to be frustrated." He has a rich style, full of imagery. *Dandelion Wine* is a beautiful coming-of-age semi–science fiction tale about twelve-year-old Douglas Spalding and a wonderful summer he has in the early nineteen hundreds. Other popular titles: *Fahrenheit 451, The Illustrated Man, The Martian Chronicles,* and *The October Country.*

Bradley, Marion Zimmer. The Darkover series. "A world where people have psychic powers. A bunch of books about this world. Each book stands by itself but they all get tied together in the end. You can jump around in the series but it's easier to read in order. Intermediate to advanced level of difficulty." Some titles: *Darkover Landfall, The Red Sun of Darkover, The Winds of Darkover.*

Brooks, Terry. His Shannara books are a popular fantasy series. "The first three were the best (*Sword of Shannara, Elfstones of Shannara,* and *Wishsong of Shannara*). I read them all in a week." One of my students described starting these books in the fourth grade: "The first one took me four weeks to read, but I really, really liked that book. Then I read all of them and got so pissed off when the series ended and I couldn't read any more." Another student commented that the theme of all of Brooks's books was "growth through challenge" but added that "you need patience" to read his series because they have so much description. He recommended less competent readers start with *Magic Kingdom For Sale—Sold!* This isn't part of a series, but is "easier to read, more fun."

Card, Orson S. This is a fairly new science fiction writer whom many of my students *love.* They are always telling me I *have* to read *Ender's Game,* the story of a brilliant young boy who prepares to save the universe by playing simulated war games. Two sequels so far: *Speaker for the Dead* and *Xenocide.* Another title that "is science fiction but doesn't seem like it" is *Songmaster.* "About a little kid who is brought up in a cold house with kids gifted in singing. Really moving and enveloping story. You get trapped in his world."

Clarke, Arthur C. Clarke is famous for using accurate science. His books call for sophisticated readers. *Rendezvous* *with Rama:* "Believable. No outrageous technology and characters have some failings." *Imperial Earth:* "Young man from one of Jupiter's moons goes to earth for the 500th anniversary celebration of the American Revolution. Experiences culture shock. Creative, believable, unexpected." Other popular titles: *2001: A Space Odyssey; Childhood's End.* "The hardest title to read is *2010;* the easiest title is *2061.*"

Cole, Adrian. The Omega series. "Some characters throughout fight an evil force that has migrated to their world from another world. Hard books but they have really good description. Really good reading."

Dicks, Terrance. Doctor Who books. "All of these are formula books, cranked out one after another. They all have the universe or a helpless race of people being threatened, the doctor always comes in in the nick of time, and through extraordinary means saves the day and vanquishes evil. They are all great. They all employ humor, general weirdness, and offbeat science fiction to form a spellbinding book." The Doctor Who books tie into a cult TV show, which is widely broadcast, and so would be a good bet for any fans of the TV series. Some titles: *Doctor Who and the Armageddon Factor, Doctor Who and the Genesis of the Daleks, Doctor Who and the Warriors of the Deep.*

Donaldson, Stephen R. *The Chronicles of Thomas Covenant, the Unbeliever.* First volume: *Lord Foul's Bane.* "He's great. I really like him a lot. About a man with leprosy who gets transported to a world where he can be healed. But he has to help the land in return."

Duncan, Dave. The Seventh Sword series. "A person gets brought from the twentieth century to an archaic world and has to figure out how to fight a group of people the residents think are sorcerers; really they just have technology. Fun books to read. For older students, but not that hard.''

*Eddings, David. Has written many fantasy series, such as The Malloreon, the Elenium, and the Belgariad. "I read them all. Great, great books. Like the Shannara books. Read in junior high. Start with the Belgariad five book series. Gets you introduced to all of the stuff Eddings does." Kids read these books up through college. "They were books I always finished. I'm a finicky fantasy reader but I don't stop halfway through these." Another avid fantasy reader told me that Eddings was absolutely the best author to introduce kids to fantasy. "Disguises being hard with fast moving plot and much dialogue. These were the books that really got me reading. I got his first six books and read them in two days."

Feist, Raymond. Riftwar Saga series. About a magician's apprentice and best friend who get taken to another world. "A really fun series to read." Medium reading skills are fine. A few of his many titles: *Magician; Magician: Apprentice; Magician: Master.*

Foster, Alan Dean. *Splinter of the Mind's Eye.* Some of my most dedicated science fiction fans tell me that this is one of the all-time best science fiction books. A wider audience likes *Aliens:* "I was reading it during seventh grade science class and I got thrown out of the class." This is another book that kids might finish after watching the movie, since the movie *Alien* is so fragmentary and evocative; the book really explains the story better—even though the book was written from the screenplay.

Forgotten Realms series. This series, published by TSR, has many different trilogies. The Avatar Trilogy is a good one to start with (by Richard Awlinson). First title: *Shadow-*

dale). Other popular series are the Icewind Dale, by R. A. Salvatore (first title: *Streams of Silver*), and the Moonshae Trilogy, by Douglas Niles (*Darkwalker on Moonshae*). More Niles titles: *Darkwell, The Kinslayer Wars, Viperhand.* These series are all fantasy. "Lots of magic, battles, bloodshed . . . The writing is always action, never a dull moment." If you have a junior high–aged boy who doesn't like to read, I'd definitely try one of these Forgotten Realm series.

Frankowski, Leo. *The Flying Warlord, The High-Tech Knight.* "About a guy who gets brought back in time to Poland, an engineer who alters the course of history. Really fun, comic, and easy."

Goldman, William. *The Princess Bride.* "About the quest for true love. Girl falls into the hands of an evil prince but her heart belongs to Westley. I was so caught up in the book my high school basketball coach came over and yelled at me during a game and told me not to read it again during a game." A fantasy novel that girls especially love.

Kay, Guy G. Writes the Fionavar Tapestry series. *The Summer Tree* is the first book. "Five college kids are taken across a time and space barrier to the world of Fionavar, which is the central world of the universe. Earth is a copy of it that went awry and is coming close to its end." Sophisticated fantasy for older readers. Newer titles: *Tigana, A Song for Arbonne.*

Heinlein, Robert. Writes science fiction that is easier to read than that of Clarke, and not as technical. "Some really nice stuff." A good writer for kids to start with. *Friday:* "What this book was really able to do is to show where the human race could be headed and why. Thoroughly enjoyable." Other titles students like include *The Door into Sum-*

mer, *Farmer in the Sky*, *The Moon Is a Harsh Mistress*, *The Puppet Masters*, and *Stranger in a Strange Land*.

Herbert, Frank. Herbert is a complex writer who writes a mixture of science fiction and fantasy. Kids either love these books or hate them. *Dune, Dune Messiah*, and *Children of Dune* are the first three of the Dune series. "Not the action packed Star Wars stuff, but more intrigue. Written almost as a history. Great books. Many wonderful philosophical ideas." Save these books for high schoolers who are good readers.

Knaak, Richard. Dragon Realm and Dragonlance series. Some titles include *Firedrake, Ice Dragon, The Black Steed*, and *Children of the Drake*. "Dragons are in control of the world but are dying off and humans are taking over. The fourth is a prehistory about how dragons took over in the first place. Don't need to read in order but can't skip around in individual books. *Kaz the Minotaur* (part of the Dragonlance series) is good to start with. It's short." Another student commented, "Really easy books, very simple."

Kurtz, Katherine. Deryni books. There are four different trilogies. "About a kingdom with two sets of people, one with magic powers and one without. The people with magic powers are persecuted." Medium reading skills.

Lawhead, Stephen R. The Dragon King trilogy. "Starts out with a little kid in the first book who helps restore a dragon king to power. Easy to read." First title: *In the Hall of the Dragon King*.

McCaffrey, Anne. Dragonflight books. This is one of the few fantasy series that feature a young woman as the main character. The books tell the story of the Dragonriders of Pern, "who fight against the Threads, and fight among themselves trying to establish civilization again." In the first book the heroine wants to become a harper, "but because of the times her father and others find it shocking for a girl to become one. The girl runs away to a cave where she becomes the owner of incredibly rare and valuable fire lizards, miniature dragons. Good book. A ten!"

Modesitt, L. E., Jr. *The Magic of Recluse* and *The Sunset Towers*. "About a boy who gets kicked out of his own country and has to figure out who he is."

Rawn, Melanie. The Dragon Prince and Dragon Star series. "The first series is about a prince coming to power but having to face lots of obstacles in his path. The Dragon Star series is about the same people but they are fighting an invading nation. Hard reading. Very long but good."

Smith, Julie Dean. *Call of Madness.* "The main character is a princess. Her father was given magic powers, but the father and the church persecute the other people with magic powers. A little more advanced than the books by Feist."

Tolkien, J.R.R. His tales of Middle Earth are probably the most popular fantasy ever written. Begin with *The Hobbit*. "*The Hobbit* is so beautiful. Not a great story but there's such great poetry in it. Sets the standard for fantasy. An everyday hero. You feel badly for the people who lose, like Gollum. He was bad, he killed things, but you felt sorry for him." *The Hobbit* is a prelude to the Lord of the Rings trilogy, which is composed of *The Fellowship of the Ring*, *The Two Towers*, and *The Return of the King*. "I tried to read these when I was young but couldn't follow them. Read them in eighth grade. Read them all. When I ran away I brought them with me—they were in a little box, and I threw the box in my bag." A very sophisticated college reader remarks: "My all-time favorite. My father read me the first part. I've reread them twice." Another reader: "Tolkien has supplementary books that are just as much fun. They tell you about all the little legends referred to in the Ring trilogy."

Weis, Margaret, and Tracey Hickman. Their Dragonlance Chronicles are "about a group of nine heroes who are trying to bring back the old gods." There are two series, the Rose of the Prophet and the Deathgate Cycle. "Must read in order. Each book is completely different; only two characters stay the same. Some characters disappear for the entire book. Have many spinoffs that are related."

Wurts, Janny. The Cycle of Fire series. "A kid comes of age and has to accept who he is. He wants to escape his father's fate of going mad. Short books that move really quickly." Titles: *Keeper of the Keys, Shadowfane.*

Zelazny, Roger. Amber Series. First title: *Nine Princes in Amber.* "For more advanced students. The books involve a lot of scheming. Relatively complicated reading but great books."

NONFICTION BOOKS

Kids tend to remember and recommend nonfiction books that are like stories. But this doesn't mean that you shouldn't buy any book you can find on subjects of passionate interest to your child. My younger daughter loves books on anatomy. She reads them over and over again—but books like this aren't really titles that kids think to recommend. Plus, their popularity depends *completely* on the reader's interest in the subject. So these nonfiction books read much more like fiction, and can be enjoyed by a wide variety of readers. But do provide your children with plenty of nonfiction books describing their area of interest.

It's also important to remember that even the books that

read like stories depend very much on the interest of the individual reader. A teenager who likes the music group U2 will find any books about that group interesting. Kids who like other groups will like other books. So look at these titles as just a random selection of the nonfiction books that one group of kids happened to like. I've divided the list into categories to help with selections.

MUSIC BIOGRAPHIES
Check out your teenager's tape and CD collection, make a note of the popular groups, and then go to the music section of a large bookstore. There's an excellent chance you'll find some books on these groups. And I'm seeing more and more that music books on the "right" groups fall into the infallible category, even with kids who literally never read. I've just listed a few of the books my kids read to give you a sense of the kinds of books I'm talking about, and to let you hear the enthusiastic voices of my students.

Alan, Carter. *Outside Is America.* "Biography of the band U2. Author's known U2 since the first show. Very interesting."

Cole, Richard. *Stairway to Heaven: Led Zeppelin Uncensored.* "About Led Zeppelin, the rise and fall of the group. I like reading anything about them. I love Led Zepplin." I had an incredibly hard time getting this student to read anything until his parents bought him this book.

Dunphy, Eamon. *Unforgettable Fire: The Definitive Biography of U2.* Another book about the band U2. "It isn't just about the band in general. It also talks about Ireland and Dublin and how growing up there affected their songs and religious beliefs." You can probably see by this quote that music books are not just for poor or mediocre readers. This extremely thoughtful, well-read young man enjoys the history and sociology found in them.

*Hopkins, Jerry, and Danny Sugerman. *No One Here Gets Out Alive.* A biography of Jim Morrison, star of The Doors. An almost infallible book for good or poor readers with an interest in music. I've seen it launch a number of boys into reading. Even if your son doesn't have a lot of Doors tapes, I might try this book. "The very well-written and interesting biography of a modern day poet, song lyricist, film maker, and all around legend that died of . . . self-abuse."

BOOKS ON DISTURBED OR TROUBLED CHILDREN
This is a very popular category with a number of my high school girls. The books by Torey Hayden, especially, have been the entry into reading for many of my students. With many of these books, it's a toss-up where you'll find them shelved. Sometimes they're in a Young Adult corner, sometimes under Psychology, sometimes under Biography—you never know. Ask before you get completely frustrated.

**Go Ask Alice.* The anonymous, true diary of a teenager who gets addicted to drugs. "Oh my God, that book is so sad. A disturbing book. I liked it but felt so bad that a girl of my age could feel things like that. A good book to get kids scared of drugs." This book, like those of S. E. Hinton, falls into the almost infallible category. I don't think I've ever had a student start this book and not finish it. Another good thing about it is the *strong* anti-drug message it carries.

Greenfield, Josh. *A Child Called Noah: A Family Journey.* A father tells the heartbreaking story of his child who isn't able to function normally. Is Noah autistic? Retarded? Greenfield explores these issues with sensitivity and passion. This book isn't as interesting to teenagers as those by Hayden or

McCracken, but mature readers are very moved by it. The sequel is titled *A Place for Noah*.

*Hayden, Torey L. Writes many books about her experiences as a special education teacher. *One Child:* "Torey's experiences as a teacher and how she got too attached to one student. Really good book. Easy reading. Sad. Once you start reading you have to finish in one sitting." *Somebody Else's Kids:* "Another class Torey has. You get involved with the students. You see how hard it is for parents to look at a child and see the disability." *Ghost Girl:* "About this girl who doesn't speak. Torey gets her to speak, and she tells these stories that make Torey believe her parents are in a Satanic cult." Other popular titles: *Just Another Kid, Murphy's Boy.* Hayden's books are also a personal favorite of mine because she so's effective in helping readers feel compassion for severely handicapped and abused children.

Levenkron, Steven. *The Best Little Girl in the World.* This is a fictionalized but very realistic account of a teenage girl who becomes anorexic. "Her parents have tried everything they could to get her to eat, but she has gotten to the point where she does not want to eat and is also afraid to eat. She was down to sixty-nine pounds and could drop dead any minute. I like it a lot. It is kind of scary." I think this is an important book for young women to read, because eating disorders are so common and so debilitating.

MacCracken, Mary. *A Circle of Children* and *Lovey.* These books describe a bored, upper-class woman whose life is changed when she volunteers to help care for emotionally disturbed children. Moderate reading skills are fine for these books. *A Circle of Children:* "It was so sad and moving. It makes me want to do what she does with kids." "*Lovey* is probably one of my favorite books of all time. I can't wonder enough how much time and energy must have been given by Mary MacCracken to the children who all had some kind of emotional handicap." MacCracken is another writer who helps sensitize readers to the plight of severely disturbed children.

O'Neill, Cherry Boone. *Starving for Attention.* The poignant, true account of Pat Boone's daughter's struggle with anorexia and bulimia.

Rubin, Theodore Isaac. *Jordi, Lisa and David:* These are fictionalized accounts of true case histories, published in the same volume. *Jordi* is a vivid, stream-of-consciousness attempt to enter the mind of a fearful, disturbed little boy. *Lisa and David* describes two disturbed teenagers. My better readers like these stories; my mediocre readers find them confusing.

Sorel, Julia. *Dawn: Portrait of a Teenage Runaway:* A girl from an abusive home runs away and is lured into prostitution. This is a short, very easy to read book that has no graphic violence or sex, in spite of its subject matter. I wouldn't even worry about giving it to junior high–aged kids; if anything, it deters runaways. My students of all reading levels really enjoy it.

COMING-OF-AGE AUTOBIOGRAPHIES AND BIOGRAPHIES
My high school students, on the whole, aren't very interested in biographies, except of sports or rock stars. The exception is my African-American students, who really seek out, and encourage me to read with them, autobiographies of black Americans.

Angelou, Maya. *I Know Why the Caged Bird Sings.* An African-American woman's very moving autobiography, describing a difficult childhood which included sexual abuse.

Her story is moving and clearly written. Average reading skills are fine.

Brown, Claude. *Manchild in the Promised Land.* Especially popular with my African-American students. "Story of a man who grows up in a negative environment but then changes himself into a positive role model. Good book for everyone." From one of my white students: "Really touching! Learned and felt a little how it would feel to grow up in Harlem."

Cary, Lorene. *Black Ice.* This is the story of Cary's experiences as a black scholarship student at the exclusive St. Paul's School in New Hampshire. My kids are just starting to discover this book, but so far all of the reports are good.

Gunther, John. *Death Be Not Proud: A Memoir.* A father tells of his son, who died at the age of eighteen of a cancerous brain tumor. "The amount of emotion and the fact that it was true made a lot of difference."

Kerouac, Jack. *On the Road.* This is a book describing the sort of wandering, hippie life-style of the sixties. It demands fairly competent reading skills, but every so often a boy comes along who really loves it. "Brought out the side of me that wants to travel and see the world and in a way satisfied those yearnings to take to the open road. Actually a miniature history lesson on a part of America's recent past."

Malcolm X, with Alex Haley. *The Autobiography of Malcolm X.* Another must try with an African-American youth. Kids with only mediocre reading skills find they can race through this book. "Malcolm X faced difficult times because he wanted to be with the crowd. When older he had a hatred toward white people, but he changed during the last few years of his life. He started to see everyone was the same. [The book is] fast because it's interesting." All of the hype about the movie has raised interest in this book but, interestingly enough, at this writing most of my African-American students have read the book but not seen the movie. And after finishing this book, some of my students go on to read other books about Malcolm X.

Wright, Richard. *Black Boy.* This is one of the most readable, accessible books by an African-American male writer. A must try for any black teenage boy you're trying to get reading, although I remember that I once had a Cambodian girl, who stayed alive scrounging single grains of rice during Pol Pot's regime, fall in love with it too. Kids are inspired by Wright's rise from poverty and abuse.

TRUE WAR AND ADVENTURE STORIES
I know there are many more good titles I'm missing here. This is a wonderful category for teenage boys, so I welcome all additions.

Caputo, Philip. *A Rumor of War.* I've had teenage boys, who've never read much of anything before, stop doing work in all of their classes to finish this book. "An exciting and informative book about Vietnam, as told by an American marine. An engrossing book about the war."

Graham, Robin L., and Derek L. Gill. *Dove.* The classic story of a sixteen-year-old boy who sails a small sloop around the world, and falls in love.

Heyerdahl, Thor. *Kon Tiki.* This is a story about crossing the Pacific Ocean by raft. An average reader can enjoy this book. My most current reader of it is a Japanese teenager who has to look up many of the words in his Japanese-American dictionary, but is determined to finish it.

Mason, Robert C. *Chickenhawk.* About the helicopter war in Vietnam. It's a pretty long, complicated book to read, and when one of my students seemed to be taking forever to finish, I kept trying to switch him to an easier book. But he was having no part of that, and regaled the class with daily updates from the war zone. I felt like *I'd* been in Vietnam. The sequel is titled *Chickenhawk: Back in the World.*

Read, Piers Paul. *Alive: The Story of the Andes Survivors.* Boys, especially ones who enjoy anything to do with the outdoors, love this book. Moderate reading skills are fine. "Awesome book. About men and their struggle against starvation and exposure. It shows how a combined effort and religion can play a part in survival. A ten!" Another comment, by a student who reads slowly and laboriously: "This is fantastic. I'm on page 73 and I've only been reading a day. It's amazing how long the survivors have been able to keep surviving." The second student became interested in this book after seeing the new movie.

Worsley, Frank Arthur. *Endurance: An Epic of Polar Adventure.* I've had a number of students enjoy this account of the work of Sir Ernest Shackleton and his men.

SPORTS BOOKS
   As in other nonfiction, there are two kinds of sports books: the instructional kind, and the story kind. Kids never mention the instructional books when I ask them about favorite reading, so I don't have any of those titles. Nevertheless, if I had a son who lived and died for basketball, I'd certainly buy him *any* books I could find on the subject, instructional or not. Kids don't read instructional books straight through, but they go back to them again and again to check out cer-

tain things. At least that's what my daughter did with her soccer books.

My sources for these lists are all kids who live around Boston, so books on Boston teams figure heavily in the recommendations. If you check local bookstores, you'll find books on teams that your sports fan roots for. Nevertheless, this list may give you an idea of the *kind* of sports books kids remember loving. Although most of these books are nonfiction, there are a couple of authors who write sports fiction whom I included here because it seemed more helpful.

Asinof, Eliot. *Eight Men Out: The Black Sox and the 1919 World Series.* This book is long, but written in the usual lively sports style. "The 1919 Black Sox scandal when they threw the World Series because of betting. The book told how everyone pulled together to fool the country and the after affects."

Bird, Larry, with Bob Ryan. *Drive: The Story of My Life.* Fast style, personal anecdotes. "Best book ever written."

Christopher, Matt. Writes many, many sports fiction books for elementary school students. A few titles: *Touchdown for Tommy, The Basket Counts, Soccer Halfback, Power Play, Centerfield Ballhawk.* A number of my students reported enjoying him. A must-try author for sports-crazy kids.

Cousy, Bob. *Cousy on the Celtic Mystique.* Cousy broadcasts the Celtics' games in Boston. "Cousy is a better author than a commentator."

Creamer, Robert W. *Babe: The Legend Comes to Life.* Although this story of Babe Ruth seems to demand good reading skills, I've watched fairly poor readers stick with it the whole way through. "A ten!"

Feinstein, John. *A Season Inside: One Year in College Basketball.* About the '87–'88 college basketball season. *Forever's Team* is about the Duke basketball teams in the late 70s and what happened to the members of the '78–'79 team that reached the finals. Also *Hard Courts: Real Life on the Professional Tennis Tours.*

Gregory, Robert. *Diz: The Story of Dizzy Dean and Baseball During the Great Depression.* The style is pretty easy flowing and a reader with moderate skills should have no trouble. "A real crazy guy. In hotels and stuff he would go crazy."

Halberstam, David. *The Summer of '49.* "About the Red Sox and Yankees' rivalry and the '49 season."

Jackson, Bo, and Dick Schaap. *Bo Knows Bo.* Easy style, first-person narrative, pictures! This book swept my lower level sophomore English class last year. "Great book about a superstar athlete and his life from childhood up."

Lamb, David. *Stolen Season: A Journey Through America and Baseball's Minor Leagues.* "A man who takes time off from *Rolling Stone* magazine, visits minor league parks and shows how difficult it is to be a minor league player. It's hard. You don't get much pay. You play every day." You could probably sell this book to your sports fan if he enjoyed the movie *Bull Durham.*

McGuane, Thomas, ed. *The Best American Sports Writing 1992.* "I enjoy sports very much and some of that stuff was great writing. One was about an awesome basketball player who was a Native American living on a reservation with his whole tribe." This book would be good for athletes who only like to read short selections. It might be the next step up from *Sports Illustrated.*

Morris, Jeannie. *Brian Piccolo: A Short Season.* "A true story about Brian Piccolo, a Chicago Bear football player who dies of cancer. Great story." If your athlete enjoys this book, you might get him *I Am Third*, by Gale Sayers with Al Silverman.

Myers, Walter Dean. Young Adult fiction author. Many titles, but my kids liked his basketball ones, which feature an African-American youth. The best: *Hoops* and *The Outside Shot:* "A story of trying to make it and the difficulties and temptations that come with it. Good story."

Okrent, Daniel, and Wulf, Steve. *Baseball Anecdotes.* Lively style. "Tells about people and events throughout the 1900s. Pretty funny and interesting. Could be good for someone who doesn't do a lot of reading." This is another book for kids who currently read only *Sports Illustrated.*

Pallone, Dave, with Alan Steinberg. *Behind the Mask: My Double Life in Baseball* This is an autobiography of a gay major league umpire. My kids enjoyed it.

Shaughnessy, Dan. *Curse of the Bambino.* "Tells why the Red Sox can't win the World Series."

Smith, Sam. *The Jordan Rules.* All about Michael Jordan. This book swept my sophomore class. The class enjoyed it because it is not complimentary to Jordan, and Jordan, of course, is a big opponent of the Celtics.

ADDENDUM TO LIST

CLASSICS RECOMMENDED OR ASSIGNED BY TEACHERS
    The purpose of this last section is to help you steer your children to the books on their summer reading lists that they'll enjoy, and to give you hints about ways to help your children with difficult reading assignments in school. Many

books that are on reading lists are already mentioned in the previous section; they've been specifically recommended to me by my students as terrific books, so I won't duplicate an entry here. What follows are authors and books that my kids don't specifically recommend, but that your child may have to read anyway.

One thing to keep in mind: many of your child's reading assignments will probably be in anthologies. This means that the older selections, which are no longer protected by copyright, may be mercilessly cut in order to remove any material remotely offensive to any group. See *What Johnny Shouldn't Read* by Joan DelFattore (Yale University Press, 1992) for a complete description of how this happens. The upshot is that the anthology selections are very boring. The Wife of Bath's Prologue in the Scott, Foresman, and Company's edition of *England in Literature* has almost all of the funny, bawdy lines missing. Their version of Pennington's slave narrative, in their *United States in Literature* text, omits all references to him being beaten or called "nigger." One wonders why he ran away! Scott, Foresman drops out a whole stanza of one of Emily Dickinson's poems, without any indication to the reader that this has been done. Authors protected by copyright have only their most inoffensive, innocuous work included.

So for any literature that has been anthologized, you may want to get a complete version for your son or daughter. The uncut versions are longer, but much more interesting and readable.

Alcott, Louisa May. *Little Women.* This nineteenth-century tale of life in Concord, Massachusetts is written in a somewhat difficult style, and is very moralistic. Nevertheless, a number of my good to excellent readers report enjoying it. (Of course, they *live* in Concord, which makes it more interesting.) I think there's an innocence to the story they find appealing. By ninth grade, even girls with average reading skill should be able to enjoy *Little Women*. Sequels: *Jo's Boys* and *Little Men*.

Beowulf. An old English folk epic that is, amazingly, taught in the sixth grade in my district. If your child is assigned it, try to get the prose translation of Burton Raffel for his homework reading assignments. The poetic ones, such as the one by Charles W. Kennedy, are much harder to follow.

Buck, Pearl S. *The Good Earth*. This is a story of life in China before the Communist Revolution. It's a very appealing story, written in a simple manner. When high school students of mine occasionally pick it up, they usually enjoy it.

Chaucer, Geoffrey. *Canterbury Tales*. Usually only one or two of his most innocent tales will be covered in a class. If your teenager is a competent reader, procure a complete version of the tales in modern English, and recommend he read the whole Wife of Bath's Prologue and the Miller's Tale. Then he'll have fond memories of Chaucer!

Cooper, James Fenimore. *The Last of the Mohicans* or *The Deerslayer* are the usual books assigned or recommended. His stories are really interesting, especially for boys, but his leisurely, fairly old-fashioned style makes his books hard to read. All but my very best readers get frustrated with his books.

Cormier, Robert. *The Chocolate War* is his most famous book, and the one that usually shows up on reading lists. My students don't warm up to his books, probably because most of his main characters are victims—of Catholic school gangs, of the government, of a fatal disease, of terrorists— whatever! But most of his books are very readable (with the exception of *I Am the Cheese*, which is pretty confusing), and so would probably keep the interest of a teenage boy with moderate reading skills.

Crane, Stephen. *The Red Badge of Courage.* This is a very short novel of the Civil War, even though Crane himself was never in that war. None of my kids really love this book, but a few of my boys find it interesting and readable. The big complaint seems to be that the main character is pretty whiny. Moderate reading skills are okay here, and the book *is* short.

Dickens, Charles. Dickens is such a leisurely writer (I think he was paid by the word) that fast readers do *much* better with him than slow readers. I love Dickens, and hate to see him ruined for kids by making them read him before they are ready. Best bets: *A Christmas Carol, A Tale of Two Cities.*

Doyle, Arthur Conan. The Sherlock Holmes mysteries. *The Hound of the Baskervilles* is the one usually assigned. Some kids with excellent reading skills really enjoy Doyle, but his old-fashioned style makes him difficult for poor or average readers. "Definitely an adult book," a fourteen-year-old, who had been assigned *Hound of the Baskervilles,* commented. Because Doyle is such a wonderful writer, and a giant of the mystery genre, I think it's too bad kids are forced to read him before they are ready.

Hawthorne, Nathaniel. Some of my girls with sophisticated reading skills enjoy *The Scarlet Letter.* It's by far the best bet of all of his books.

Homer. *The Iliad* and *The Odyssey.* The translation is everything here. Make sure your children have a clear prose translation if they need to read Homer. Richard Lattimore has a breathtakingly beautiful poetic translation, but save it until your kids are in graduate school.

Melville, Herman. *Moby Dick* is his best and most famous. I've had kids enjoy reading parts of it, but I've never had anyone go the whole way through. *Billy Budd*, a much shorter novel about a sailor on a British man-of-war, is often taught, but even the best readers find it difficult, mostly because of Melville's old-fashioned style. There is a movie version available.

Paton, Alan. *Cry, the Beloved Country* is the usual book taught or put on reading lists. It's a stunningly beautiful book about South Africa. Unfortunately, all but the best readers find it confusing. Another book of Paton's, *Too Late the Phalarope*, is even more moving and shocking but again, it's only for excellent readers. (I've tried and tried and tried teaching *Too Late the Phalarope* to average readers but haven't been successful. I'm afraid I've just taught many teenagers to dislike Paton.)

Plath, Sylvia. *The Bell Jar.* This is a vivid, semi-autobiographical account of Sylvia Plath's suicide attempt that she made one summer when she was a college student. Boys have trouble feeling sympathy for Plath's main character, Esther Greenwood. Girls, even those with just moderate reading skills, find the book engrossing but depressing. The subject matter is too depressing, I think, for anyone under the age of fifteen or sixteen. Even then I'd be careful, because the book is so well written that Plath really makes the reader feel what she is feeling.

Poe, Edgar Allan. Poe's short stories have wonderful, creepy plots but are written in a very complex style. See if your teenager will let you read the story aloud to him. If so, read it in a scary voice. Ham it up! *The Cask of Amontillado* is wonderful heard aloud.

Shakespeare. Shakespeare is wonderful, of course, but very difficult for almost all young people to read. There's no getting around that fact. So the edition is everything here. You want to find one with little scene summaries and excellent notes. My favorite editions are the Folger ones. If your child has a choice of Shakespearean plays, suggest *Romeo and Juliet* or *Hamlet* (even though it's long). There are excellent movie versions of these two, and both have young people as their main characters. Show the movie first. While your teenager is reading the play, it's helpful if you can find a good complete tape or record version. It's much easier to follow the play if professional actors are reading the lines.

Wilde, Oscar. *The Importance of Being Earnest.* This is one of my all-time favorite plays, but I've found that kids need to be good readers and have a pretty sophisticated sense of humor to enjoy it. There is an excellent movie version of this.

Wilder, Thornton. *Our Town.* I had the best success with *Our Town* this year when I did the play with my high school juniors. They really liked and understood it; I think usually it's taught to kids who are too young. If your younger child is assigned the play, you might ask if you can read it with him. Take parts, and let him have all the best ones.

INDEX